PRAISE FOR *HABAKKUK*

Who would imagine that a tiny Old Testament book, written by a prophet whose name most of us can't pronounce would be relevant to the trials of our current day? Dannah Gresh dusts off this ancient treasure and brings to life the promises that you and I must cling to in times of fear, wrestling, silence, and tragedy.

JULI SLATTERY
Author and cofounder, Authentic Intimacy

I've known Dannah Gresh for over thirty years, and this study reverberates with her heart for Christ's church. Her challenge to us, like Habakkuk's, is to wake up and listen for God's voice, to be watchmen for Him in the time in which we live, and to make Christ's glory known to the nations.

DONNA VANLIERE
Speaker and author of *The Time of Jacob's Trouble*

We love control, and when we do not understand what God is doing, we get impatient and forget God's promises. What do we do with our fears and doubts? Can we wrestle with God when He seems silent? Dannah takes us through an in-depth study of the book of the prophet Habakkuk and the historical context surrounding it. She encourages us to remember God's faithfulness in the past, trust that He is working in the present, and watch and wait for His deliverance. This is a great resource to help us grow in our faith when we forget to remember. Very recommended for individual study or group settings!

LAURA GONZALEZ DE CHAVEZ
Director, Aviva Nuestros Corazones

Dannah provides an invaluable journey studying the book of Habakkuk. You will gain crucial foundation stones on which to build your relationship with your Heavenly Father. You will be taken deeper into His unfailing love, learning how to have a praying life that is intimate and real. Your faith will soar and your fears diminish as you learn to walk the path of faith.

FERN NICOLS
Author and founder, Moms In Prayer International

We all want to be astounded by God. But can we find wonder in His silence? In His discipline? Do we believe that God is good when nothing else seems to be? These are the questions we find embedded in the ancient prophetic book Habakkuk and the questions that Dannah Gresh writes us a permission slip to wrestle with in this breathtaking study. Dannah has walked the road of devastation and emerged astounded by God's grace. Let her be your guide as you take God's Word into the deepest places of your heart.

ERIN DAVIS
Author, podcaster, and Bible teacher

Other Studies by Dannah Gresh from Moody Publishers

For Teens
And the Bride Wore White: Seven Secrets to Sexual Purity

Lies Young Women Believe: and the Truth That Sets Them Free
(Cowritten with Nancy DeMoss Wolgemuth)

For Tweens & Their Moms
Lies Girls Believe: and the Truth That Sets Them Free
(Edited by Nancy DeMoss Wolgemuth)

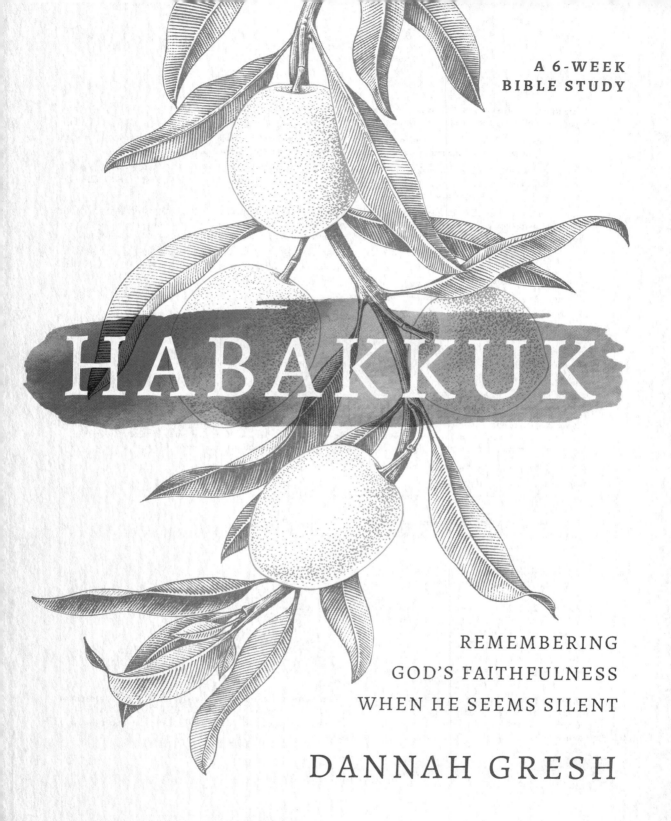

A 6-WEEK
BIBLE STUDY

HABAKKUK

REMEMBERING
GOD'S FAITHFULNESS
WHEN HE SEEMS SILENT

DANNAH GRESH

MOODY PUBLISHERS
CHICAGO

Edited by Amanda Cleary Eastep
Interior and Cover Design: Erik M. Peterson
Cover illustration of olives copyright © 2019 by channarongsds / Adobe Stock (210505982). All rights reserved.

All websites and phone numbers listed herein are accurate at the time of publication but may change in the future or cease to exist. The listing of website references and resources does not imply publisher endorsement of the site's entire contents. Groups and organizations are listed for informational purposes, and listing does not imply publisher endorsement of their activities.

Library of Congress Cataloging-in-Publication Data

Names: Gresh, Dannah, 1967- author.
Title: Habakkuk : remembering God's faithfulness when he seems silent /
   Dannah Gresh.
Description: Chicago : Moody Publishers, 2020. | Includes bibliographical
   references. | Summary: «Learn how the storms of life can become
   opportunities to activate your faith in Habakkuk: Remembering the
   Faithfulness of God When He Seems Silent. Through daily Scripture,
   prayer, and meditation, this six-week study will teach you how to
   remember that God is at work-even when He seems silent»-- Provided by
   publisher.
Identifiers: LCCN 2020013646 (print) | LCCN 2020013647 (ebook) | ISBN
   9780802419804 (paperback) | ISBN 9780802498731 (ebook)
Subjects: LCSH: Bible. Habakkuk--Textbooks.
Classification: LCC BS1635.52 .G74 2020 (print) | LCC BS1635.52 (ebook) |
   DDC 242/.5--dc23
LC record available at https://lccn.loc.gov/2020013646
LC ebook record available at https://lccn.loc.gov/2020013647

Originally delivered by fleets of horse-drawn wagons, the affordable paperbacks from D. L. Moody's publishing house resourced the church and served everyday people. Now, after more than 125 years of publishing and ministry, Moody Publishers' mission remains the same—even if our delivery systems have changed a bit. For more information on other books (and resources) created from a biblical perspective, go to: www.moodypublishers.com or write to:

Moody Publishers
820 N. LaSalle Boulevard
Chicago, IL 60610

3 5 7 9 10 8 6 4 2

Printed in the United States of America

To my mother, Kay Barker,
who prayed Habakkuk 1:5 over my life.

CONTENTS

Part 2: How to Hear God Through the Hurt

We were created for community. And because of that, I hope you'll enjoy this Bible study with a small group. My website—dannahgresh.com—contains the following support mechanisms for your group experience:

- a podcast series with weekly content to kick off your week.
- videos of our podcast recording, should you prefer that format.
- a downloadable leader's guide

When you meet weekly with other women, you can discuss ideas and concepts and gain more insight from the Lord about what to do with what you are learning from His Word.

Whether you do this on your own or in a group, you'll be utilizing the powerful skill of meditation throughout this study. Habakkuk models it beautifully. Allow me just a few moments to introduce the concept to you.

WHAT IS MEDITATION?

Many years ago, a pastor invited me to start meditating as a part of my daily quiet time with God. He explained it this way: Some people are very rigid about studying the Bible, and others are quite committed to praying, but few combine the power of these two effectively.

MEDITATION IS WHAT HAPPENS WHEN STUDYING AND PRAYING COLLIDE.

The goal is to have a strong balance of both in your life. When you do, you engage in a two-way conversation with God. And that's the whole point of prayer—to tell God how you are feeling and what you need, but also to listen to Him and learn from Him. This study will help you maintain mindfulness concerning both elements in your ongoing conversation with God.

I've divided your daily assignments into two sections: studying and praying. When you have completed both activities each day, you have meditated. Time is a necessary part of the meditation process. Don't rush the experience if you truly want to have a good conversation with God.

Plan to invest about twenty-five to forty minutes each day, depending on your personal pace.

When I began research for this Bible study, I could not have imagined the backdrop upon which it would be released. On my very last day of writing, I heard of a deadly novel corona-virus infecting people in China. It quickly spread to break national health care systems, empty public spaces, crash economies, and leave once-powerful clusters of urban activity silenced in grief. Before we sent this book to the printer, the COVID-19 pandemic had imprinted the world. We need the lessons of Habakkuk always, but in an urgent and desperate way right now.

The book of Habakkuk, named after its author, is about learning to believe that God is good and maintains control even when there is so much evil and tragedy in the world around us. Though this book is often overlooked during times of peace and prosperity, it has tended to be studied when believers needed to learn how to talk to God during epic and evil events, such as World War II.

Habakkuk's book starts with fear and questions about the broken world in which the prophet lives. But you and I will have front-row seats to watch a man who was shaken by the evil and suffering in the world progress to become a shining example of how the righteous live by faith.

Here's what I believe studying Habakkuk will do for you.

- You'll gain perspective on the trials you're currently facing—whether they be large or small—and learn how to navigate them free of fear and full of joy.
- You'll exercise six habits of living by faith.
- You'll remember how God has been faithful to you in the past.
- You'll be prepared to face the trials you're facing now or will in the future.
- You'll learn how to talk to God during hard times.
- God will—I did not say may—extend or expand a special invitation to you concerning the trials of others, including other people groups and nations.
- And He could revive you.

Those are the things God did for me as I studied Habakkuk. I'm filled with expectancy that God will do the same things in you.

In His Great Love,

Dannah
January 2020, The Gresh Farm
(Revised April 2020 on my fourteenth day of self-quarantine)

PART ONE

How to Pray When You're Devastated

During Part 1, you'll be learning how to talk to God when your heart is hurting. This first portion is loaded with important background study on the book of Habakkuk. Expect to spend the majority of your time studying and a shorter amount of time praying each day.

Why Would I Want to Study Habakkuk?

Your experience in these pages will be greatly enhanced by listening to teaching podcasts to kick off each week. The six-session podcast series can be found at dannahgresh.com on my podcast page under the series *Habakkuk: Remembering God's Faithfulness When He Seems Silent.* Each is also available as video for group study. The lessons you'll glean from the podcasts are important to this study, but you will still be able to do the study if you're not able to listen to the podcasts.

Habakkuk means to _____ or _____.[1]

THE POWER OF HABAKKUK'S POETRY

1. Poetry requires us to get _____ with _____.

2. Poetry is _____ with _____.

3. Poetry is _____.

4. The _____ _____ poetry requires results in _____ _____.

5. Poetry helps us _____.

OTHERS WHO THOUGHT HABAKKUK WAS POWERFUL

1. _____ wanted it _____.

2. The _____ _____ used it as the _____ of _____ _____.

3. _____ _____ used it to get through _____ _____.

Habit #1: Remember to wrestle with God when He seems silent.

Answers to the podcast fill-in-the-blanks can be found on page 215.

WEEK 1

Remember to Wrestle

"This feels like another hard season that we're in. [I have an] uneasy feeling of fear and dread. This world continually reminds us that the unthinkable happens."

My friend Leila wrote that on her daughter Julie's 683rd day battling leukemia.

She admits it was getting harder to remember the faith they had on day number one—diagnosis day.

But God has a way of swooping in to help us with our amnesia.

For Leila, He showed up with a special reminder on day number 669. She was at a greater New York City area support group for cancer moms. One of them shared the story of her son's diagnosis day. In the middle of all the bad news, there was—she reported with tears—a Bible verse hanging on her son's inpatient room when they arrived. Not just any Bible verse. One of their favorites.

> Have I not commanded you? Be strong and courageous. Do not be frightened, and do not be dismayed, for the LORD your God is with you wherever you go.
> (JOSH. 1:9)

It was just the reminder they needed. They weren't in that hospital room alone. God was with them. He had been there before them to plant a much-needed reminder of faith and hope.

Leila had to ask: *Which hospital? Which room?* But she already knew the answers.

Morristown.

Room 10.

Her daughter Julie had written that verse on a piece of paper and stuck it to the wall, but when she'd been urgently moved late in the night, the verse was left behind. And no one took it down . . . after one full year.

"It was a powerful moment for both of us. A good reminder that even though times seem tough, God has not left us, and will not leave us," wrote Leila. Her faith refreshed. Renewed. Rekindled as they continue to count the days.

Today is day number 714.

Maybe you too struggle with forgetting to remember. I'm here to remind you.

MEDITATION 1

Forgetting to remember

People say that God is never late. I say that He sure seems slow sometimes.

Why doesn't He answer your prayers to bring you someone to share your life with or someplace to call home? The medical breakthrough that could bring you a new lease on life or the help you need when you've been biting off more than you can chew?

When is He going to show up with the answer you need or the money you owe? Or to fix what's wrong in the church or avenge the one who wronged you in your family?

Where is He when your daughter's fighting cancer or you're fumbling your career? When you're at the end of your rope or the beginning of a terrifying storm?

Sometimes God seems so unbelievably silent. This seems especially true in the storms of our life.

Are you in a storm of some kind?

I'm here to help you not to forget to remember.

We tend to do that in times of downpour. The disciples did. One day Jesus got into a boat with them, and said He wanted to go to the other side of a lake.[2] Then He fell asleep. That's when a windstorm came down on them. It must have been a whopper, because the boat began to take on water. What started out as a merry version of *Row, Row, Row Your Boat* turned into the theme song for *Titanic*.

And Jesus slept right through it.

Feel familiar?

The seasoned fishermen shook. You'd better believe they woke the weary Teacher up: Jesus, we're dying! Don't You care?

He did care, and He told the wind and the raging waves so.

Then He turned His attention back to the guys in the boat. He had something to say to them too. There, in the calm of yet another miracle, He asks them: Where is your faith?

Not the most comforting thing to say to a few grown men who'd probably just lost their lunch about the time they lost their cool. But Jesus doesn't stroke their egos, as we are prone to do. Instead, He cuts to the chase, essentially asking: Did you forget who I Am? Did you forget Who is with you?

They had, in fact, forgotten who was with them. In spite of all the amazing things they had been witness to, the men cowered when a storm brewed.

Can you identify?

If so, Habakkuk is just the tutor we both need. Oh, at the beginning of his three-chapter book, he doesn't seem to be. In fact, he's dreadfully afraid of the future and seems to be the poster child for doubt, fear, and questioning God. He has a big case of spiritual amnesia. But by the end of the book, his memory kicks in and he becomes a shining example of how the righteous live by faith. And so much of faith has to do with remembering.

**REMEMBER
(re•member)**

verb. Have in or be able to bring to one's mind an awareness of (someone or something that one has seen, known, or experienced in the past).[3]

I once heard that to remember is "to put back what is dismembered."[4] Much as you would reattach a limb if it were tragically lost, hopelessness requires us to re-member what's been missing in our minds and souls.[5] We're invited to put our faith back where it belongs.

In this study, we will discover the six practices or habits Habakkuk exercised to re-member his faith.

Shall we get started?

Today, I'm providing the passage we'll be studying right here in the English Standard Version. I encourage you to mark up your Bible when you're learning as I have in the sample below.

Our study activities today and tomorrow are based on the center of Habakkuk, where we find the thesis for the book. Begin by reading and writing out any early observations you have about Habakkuk 2:2–3 either below or in your own Bible.

The Righteous Shall Live by His Faith

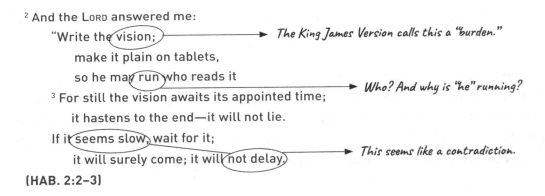

² And the Lord answered me:
    "Write the vision; ──────────────► *The King James Version calls this a "burden."*
        make it plain on tablets,
        so he may run who reads it
³ For still the vision awaits its appointed time; ──────► *Who? And why is "he" running?*
        it hastens to the end—it will not lie.
    If it seems slow, wait for it;
        it will surely come; it will not delay. ──────► *This seems like a contradiction.*
    (HAB. 2:2–3)

Given the facts that this book is written in poetry and poetry requires us to seek after its meaning, what's ironic about the first sentence God speaks to Habakkuk in this passage?

There is nothing plain about the poetry of Habakkuk. So, this is not speaking of the style of writing, rather the intention of it.

The New International Version reads: "'Write down the revelation and make it plain on tablets so that a herald may run with it.'" A herald is an official messenger assigned to bring news about something.

What can we assume if God is expecting Habakkuk to send someone running with this "plain" message?

What did God instruct Habakkuk to write the message on?

Of course, we have a lot of ancient documents and forms of communication carved on tablets, but as early as 1500 BC, scrolls of papyrus, parchment, or leather were other common methods of writing and a bit less tedious than carving on stone or wood tablets. It's likely that Habakkuk was using the latter. It was a unique instruction that stands out in the pages of Scripture. Only a few other writers recorded similar specific instructions from God about the messages He gave them. Moses records that the Ten Commandments were written on stone tablets (Ex. 24:12). Isaiah reveals that he wrote his beautiful prophecy of Christ's birth on wood tablets (Isa. 30:8). And Job reveals that he recorded wisdom on a rock concerning how to suffer (Job 19:24).

What might we assume based on the fact that Habakkuk is instructed to write this on tablets rather than on scrolls?

Why might these authors, including Habakkuk, have been specifically instructed to use tablets rather than easier methods of inscription?

Having these books written on more durable materials communicates that God wanted these messages to last. Why? Habakkuk 2:3 may offer us some clues.

What promises about the revelation does God make? And what will they require of Habakkuk?

When I read this verse, I wanted to point out conflict in stating that Habakkuk had to "wait for it," and that it "will not delay." It seems God often asks us to wait, especially when we are facing painful storms in our lives.

Read James 1:2–4. Why does God allow us to wait patiently for Him to show up in our times of need?

Oh, if only God offered us immediate results for our prayer requests and did not make us dust off our patience, dig up some steadfast staying power, and muster up our joy! But He often takes us through monsoon seasons that require those very things of us. Often when we come out the other side, we see that God has used it to help us remember our faith.

● ● ●

When Jesus stilled the wind and raging waters that day on the lake for the fearful fishermen, He used it to invite them to remember what they'd lost for a moment. Luke records that the Savior asked them: *Where is your faith?*

He didn't ask: *Don't you have any faith?*

He knew they had it. I imagine Him asking them this in the same tone He might have asked them, *Well, where were your raincoats? Don't you think they could have been helpful in this situation?*

This was just the prompting they needed to remember. They turned to one another and said, *Who is this!? Even the winds and water obey Him!*

The question is not answered, but one is implied: *God is with us!*

Whatever "wind" and "water" you're facing in your storm, I assure you of this: God is with you. Even if you've forgotten to remember that.

For today's prayer activity, imagine that Jesus has been sleeping in your proverbial storm, whatever that may be. Write what you would say to awaken Him. And then imagine He asks you, "Where is your faith?" What would you tell Him? Do you need to remember? Write a prayer in the space below.

MEDITATION 2

*Are you living
by faith or fear?*

"Noah believed in rain before *rain* was a word."[6]

That sentence stopped me dead in my tracks recently.

And it's not just because when I get to heaven, I want to see Jesus and *then* Mrs. Noah. Animal lover that I am, it has always been on my bucket list to have tea with her and thank her for helping God save all those lovely creatures. But more than that, she was one amazing woman of faith.

Burdened by the broken condition of the world, Noah and his wife had faith that God would fix things. They did not fixate on the chaos around them; they kept their minds tuned in to the God they trusted. They reacted with faith instead of fear. They built a boat. A big one. Even though they'd never seen a drop of rain.

Until recently, I had not considered the absolute insanity of that kind of faith. Crazy as it seemed, Noah built an ark proving his faith in God.

Is your world looking a little broken? Or a lot?

Do you need some "rain" in your life?

Do you have the faith to believe God will send it? And to live as if you believe it?

Or are you struggling to even believe that God is up there? Or that He is good?

You're in just the right place, my friend.

Habakkuk was struggling to believe that God was up there too.

But by the time he gets midway through his storm, he has remembered what was lost.

Today, we'll complete our study in the center of Habakkuk, and we will examine the thesis for the book. Begin by reading and making notes about your observations for Habakkuk 2:4 in your Bible.

What phrase or line in the poetry is familiar because you've read it in other parts of the Bible or heard it spoken frequently? Look up Romans 1:17 and Galatians 3:11 to see how the apostle Paul quoted Habakkuk. Then, look up Hebrews 10:38 to see how the author of Hebrews referenced it. Write the key phrase below.

Let's start this study with a good solid definition of faith.

From a faith perspective, our confidence and trust rests in God.

FAITH
(feyth)

noun. Confidence or trust in a person or thing.[7]

Look up Hebrews 11:1. Based on this verse, write your own definition of faith below.

Hebrews 11:1–40 honors individuals of exemplary faith.

Read Hebrews 11:13, which is no doubt another spot where the author was referencing Habakkuk. Answer the following questions.

How were these people living when they died?

Why did they have to continue that way?

But they still "saw" the things they hoped for. How?

What did this make them feel like?

Believing in the God of the universe and all of His promises can make you feel like a stranger. But those who walk by faith keep believing until the moment they are called "home."

How has living by faith made you feel like an alien or stranger in your own corner of the world?

I've listed a few of the "card-carrying members of the Hall of Faith" below. These are not people who just said they believed something. They acted on what they believed.

Skim Hebrews 11:1–40. What was the specific thing that each of the people below "had not yet seen," making their faith worthy of mention? You'll need to draw on your understanding of these key Bible characters. I've included the passage where their story originally appears in case you want to reference it.

CARD CARRYING MEMBER OF THE HALL OF FAITH	WHAT THEY HAD NOT YET SEEN
Noah (Gen. 6:9–9:17)	Rain
Abraham (Gen. 12–25)	
Sarah (Gen. 12–23)	
Joseph (Gen. 37–50)	

A home and sense of belonging. Babies. Deliverance from human trafficking and abuse. Children who walk with God. Maybe the greats of the faith longed for some of the same things we do.

There's another thing we have in common with them. They lived in a broken world full of broken people surviving broken dreams.

So do we.

As we get to know Habakkuk and those his writing impacted, our own experiences of fear and faith will be validated or re-directed through Scripture. Our faith will be remembered as we examine how God has worked on behalf of others.

When you learn how God has worked throughout history, you can depend on His working in a similar way with you.
—HENRY T. BLACKABY AND CLAUDE V. KING[8]

That brings me back to Noah. It was a dark time to be alive. The Bible states that people were violent and corrupt (Gen. 6:5). It is not difficult to imagine a world where murder and war were the norm. Only eight people were chosen by God to harbor inside the ark (1 Peter 3:20). The rest were so completely depraved that you and I may have a hard time imagining it.

Noah—like every other individual in the Hall of Faith—could have focused on all the pain he saw around him. He lived in anxious, fearful times. But he did not wear his hurt. He wore his hope.

He chose faith over fear. Will you?

● ● ●

To prepare for today's prayer activity, I want to invite you to take inventory of your own life. This is a long assignment. I want to be thorough about pinpointing your need as we get started. Are you living by faith? Or are you living by fear? Answer the questions prayerfully.

LIVING BY FAITH

Below are some of the evidences and outcomes of faith. Check the ones that are true of you. The questions below each category are to help you consider it carefully.

_____**YOU ARE JUSTIFIED IN CHRIST AND SAVED**
(Eph. 2:8; John 3:16; Rom. 10:9)
  • Are you mindful of your sin and aware of its impact?
  • Was there a time in your life that you were sure that Christ lived, died, and rose again? Did you confess it with your mouth to others? Are you "saved"?
  • Is there evidence in your life that Christ has changed you? Has your confession of faith proven to be genuine? Do you live free from the shame of your sin and in full joy of your salvation?

_____**YOU EXPERIENCE ANSWERS TO YOUR PRAYERS**
(Matt. 17:20; 15:28; Mark 11:24)
  • Do you take your burdens, complaints, and woes to God? Do you seek answers from Him?
  • When was the last time you felt God answered a prayer with a clear yes, no, or wait?
  • Can you recount stories in your life where God showed up to rescue you or those you love?

_____ **YOU HAVE PEACE AND JOY**
(Rom. 5:1; Isa. 26:3; James 1:2–4; Phil. 4:4–9)
  • Even though there are trials in your life, is the overall tenor of your spirit peaceful? When you face difficult times, do you remain largely peaceful?

• Do you have a sense that even difficult things will strengthen your faith and perfect you as an individual?

• Do you choose to rejoice when circumstances are difficult, resulting in a shift in your emotions? Are you certain that God is in control of everything?

_____YOU HAVE THE ABILITY TO OVERCOME AND LIVE VICTORIOUSLY IN CHRIST

(Eph. 6:16; 1 John 5:4; John 1:5)

• Do you have an awareness of the battle between good and evil? And do you sense that you have power to overcome the darkness through faith and prayer?

• Though you sometimes feel tempted, is your life lived in the direction of moral purity and holiness, as opposed to generally succumbing to sinful desires?

_____YOU LIVE SURRENDERED TO CHRIST

(Heb. 11:8; Jer. 29:11)

• Have you surrendered your life purpose to God? Are you doing what He has created you, equipped you, and prepared you to do with your life? Are you aware that He has a good plan, even if you cannot see exactly what it is or how it unfolds?

• Do you sense the joy of living your life in obedience to God? Are you aware that your paycheck is heavenly and intangible? Are you certain you have an inheritance?

_____YOU HAVE CONFIDENCE ABOUT THE FUTURE

(Heb. 11:1; Prov. 31:25; 2 Cor. 5:7; Rom. 8:28)

• Do you look to the future with happiness and joy? Do you laugh (as opposed to cry) about what's ahead?

• Do you feel hopeful when you think about the future? Even if things aren't all going in the direction you'd planned, do you sense that God is at work and will bring something good out of where you are?

LIVING BY FEAR

Below are some of the evidences and outcomes of fear. Check any of them that are true of you.

_____ **YOU FEEL LIKE YOU ARE NOT A PART OF GOD'S FAMILY**
(Rom. 11:20; Heb. 4:2; 11:6)
• Do you feel like you don't fit in or don't belong around church or around Christian people?
• Do you doubt God's existence? Do you struggle to understand the words you read in the Bible?
• Do you feel cut off or rejected from people at church even when they are warm and welcoming to you?
• Have you made a conscious decision that you are not a Christian?

_____ **YOU GENERALLY FEEL YOUR PRAYERS ARE NOT ANSWERED**
(Matt. 13:58; 21:22; Mark 11:24; James 1:6; 4:3)
• Do you feel like God does not hear your prayers? Are you disappointed with the number of times you can remember feeling like God answered your prayers?
• Are your motives often built on your selfish desires rather than on faith-filled promises?

_____ **YOU EXPERIENCE A GREAT DEAL OF FEAR AND ANXIETY**
(John 14:1–2; 2 Tim. 1:7; Ps. 32:10)
• Do you struggle with overwhelming or constant fear and anxiety (as opposed to occasional)? Is your natural state of reaction to the future fearful?
• Do you react fearfully towards others during difficult times, rather than responding with self-control and love and peace?
• As a general rule, do you live under the weight of a sick heart? Do you feel weighed down by anxiety? Do you have a hard time remembering that God has a good plan?

_____**YOU'RE LIVING IN BONDAGE TO ADDICTION AND SIN**

(Heb. 3:12, 13; Rom. 4:20)

• Do you seem to be powerless over sin, even when you know it's wrong? Is there a recurring sinful habit or pattern that you have been unable to break?

• Do you no longer even feel convicted about behavior that you know is bad for you or is called sin in the Bible? Is your heart growing hard?

• Have you begun to doubt that God can even forgive you?

_____**YOU SUFFER FROM A LACK OF PURPOSE AND DIRECTION**

(James 1:5, 6; Heb. 10:36)

• Are you having a hard time discovering your life's purpose? Do you feel like you are tossed to and fro in various directions without a solid compass to direct you?

• Do you feel like giving up? Are you prone to forget what God has promised you in His word about your purpose and future? Have you forgotten entirely?

_____**YOU HAVE NO ENTHUSIASM ABOUT THE FUTURE**

(Prov. 12:25; 3:5-6)

• Is your natural state of reaction about the future negative?

• Do you lean on your own understanding of the future without applying God's Truth and direction to your path in life?

• As a general rule, do you live under the weight of a sick heart? Do you have a hard time remembering that God is unfolding a good plan?

Based on what you sensed God saying as you prayed through this inventory, are you living primarily in faith or predominantly in fear? Write a prayer to God, communicating what you would like Him to help you change.

MEDITATION 3

When was the last time you heard from God?

As I pound out these words on a computer, another year is coming to a close and it's official: the number one highlighted, shared, and looked-up verse of the year is a healing balm for anxiety and fear.[9]

> Do not be anxious about anything, but in everything by prayer and supplication with thanksgiving let your requests be made known to God.
> (PHIL. 4:6)

What are you afraid of right now? I bet there is something. The future. The bills. An old wound. An addiction. Spending your life alone. Spending your energy in a purposeless career.

Everything in me wants to tell you, *"It's going to be okay."*

But that platitude will make you weak. It will lull you into comfortable complacency. God knows you were made for more. So, let me tell you the truth.

First, in all likelihood, what's ahead is going to be so much harder than you can imagine. Of course, that's not a guarantee. Sometimes we get a bye.

The second thing you need to know is this: If you can learn to live in faith rather than fear, it's going to be so much more amazing than you can imagine. And that I can promise you.

God wants to strengthen you for what's ahead. He wants the muscles of your emotions, your mind, and your will to be trained for walking in the most difficult places.

So, I'm not going to tell you what you want to hear. I'm going to take you to God's Word and invite God's Spirit to tell you what you need to hear. And we'll use the ancient writing of the prophet Habakkuk to turn up the volume.

For today's study activity, I'd like you to become better acquainted with Habakkuk. You'll quickly see that you may have some things in common with him. Begin by reading and making observations about Habakkuk 1:1a.

Say the name of the writer of this book out loud.

Just kidding! No one knows how to pronounce Habakkuk. Just have confidence when you say it. You're probably saying it wrong, but so is everyone else!

What title does he use?

The book of Habakkuk is a vision the prophet receives from God. In the original Hebrew, this word is rooted in the noun *hazon,* which means "vision, revelation."[10]

Many years ago, my husband Bob was burdened by the pressure he was receiving from some people to write a long-term strategic plan that encapsulated his vision for Grace Prep, a Christian high school we founded together. While he and I both feel it can be useful to have a mission statement and some short-term objectives, we often see churches and ministries pursue human-centered ideas rather than God-sized tasks. Our own plans often get in the way of our ability to see God's plans.

Bob asked God for wisdom, and the Lord directed him to this Bible verse. (Excuseth the King James. It's what my husband groweth up on.)

Where there is no vision, the people perish: but he that keepeth the law, happy is he.
(PROV. 29:18 KJV)

Circle the English version of the word hazon *(meaning vision or revelation) in that verse. Then, double underline the outcome of living without it.*

How might someone living without vision (or revelation) "perish"? What might they experience?

If you are not hearing from God concerning the direction of your future, you will grow dispassionate, disinterested, and disgruntled no matter how many good ideas you have. You and I need to hear from God. We need *hazon*. Our emotional and spiritual heartbeat grows faint if we are not directed by Him. Purpose fades. Hope dies. And before long, we're forgetting to remember.

Ironically, one important element that calls us into our future is our past. So much about what God has ahead for us is tied to what God has already done! Therefore, we must remember. Treasuring what God has done in our past helps us make it through difficult times and hope in what God can do in the future.

I find that we know this in our heads. However, when times get difficult, we often forget to remember what God has already done in our lives. To help us embrace this, we'll be plotting Habakkuk's timeline. By the end of our study, we'll have charted his past, present, and future in an effort to build our own faith.

TIME FOR TIMELINES!
Turn to pages 222–223 in the back of the book.

You'll discover a two-page timeline spread. We're going to begin to plot important dates, names, and events for the nation of Judah to gain perspective as we study this book. A lot of the stuff that happens on the timeline of Jewish history gives us context to fill in layers of meaning within the author's poetry. Let's get the first two recorded right now.

Find 930 BC on the timeline and note how I've handwritten, "Israel Divides."[11]

This is a somewhat significant event in the history of Israel. I found that plotting on the timeline helped me to see when Israel was one nation and when it had divided. The Northern half retained the name Israel and comprised ten tribes. The Southern half was called Judah and included the other two tribes, which retained the sacred land of Israel. Habakkuk's prophecy concerned the nation of Judah.

Find the bar that runs from 612 BC to 588 BC and write "Habakkuk."[12]

Habakkuk's ministry began in 612 BC and ended about 588 BC. Sometime between those bookends of our prophet's life, he wrote his poetry for us. And he's pretty worked up when he does. Why? The King James Version makes it a bit easier to see.

Circle the word that the KJV uses in place of the English Standard Version's oracle.

"The burden which Habakkuk the prophet did see."
(HAB. 1:1)

To Habakkuk, God seemed silent. That would have probably been stressful for a man who had been chosen by God to carry His *hazon* to the people. For that reason alone, the prophet could have been burdened, but there was a reason God was silent. He was frustrated with His people.

And so was Habakkuk. He was deeply disturbed with the sins of the Jewish people, which we'll look at specifically in Meditation 4. The state of the nation was impacting him personally, and there would be more suffering to come. Unfortunately for Habakkuk, he was a prophet. So he knew it. If we peeked at the end of his book, we'd essentially see the Great Depression meeting an ancient World War. No wonder he's burdened.

A few synonyms for burden *are listed below. Circle any that seem all too familiar to you concerning what you just recorded.*

Anxiety	Hardship	Grievance
Concern	Load	Obstruction
Difficulty	Affliction	Sorrow
Stress	Purposelessness	Depression

What burden are you currently suffering under? What is it that you have but do not want? What do you want, but do not have? Where do you need hazon?

In the next few days, we'll examine what Habakkuk did with his burden. We have a clue in the meaning of his name.

Look back at your notes from this week's podcast if you don't recall the meaning of Habakkuk's name. How are these two actions alike, but different?

Does Habakkuk wrestle with God or embrace Him when He seems silent? Tomorrow we'll find out. In the meantime, do you wish God would not be so silent? Tell Him.

When was the last time you really felt like you heard God's revelation of Truth in the depths of your being? Are you craving answers and direction from Him? Write a prayer to God below.

● ● ●

MEDITATION 4

Why, God?

Jesus promised that faith the size of a mustard seed would move mountains (Matt. 17:20). He said that if we ask anything in His name, He would do it for us (John 14:13). The Bible says that when two or three are gathered, He is there with us (Matt. 18:20).

So why did my horses break the pasture fence this morning while I'm trying to write this book and Bob's way off in Cuba where he cannot help me?

Why does Communism thrive?

Why are little girls often prey to the lust of men and forced to keep secrets?

Why does Julie have cancer? Why can't God lead us to a cure?

Why did my friend Kerry die?

Why, God?

Those are some of the thoughts assaulting my study time today. I wonder, what's distracting you? Never be afraid of the thoughts assaulting you when you are about to spend time with God. They may be the very thing He wants you to bring to Him during your time together.

Whatever is on your mind, bring it into this study today.

Let's further examine Habakkuk's burden and validate his fear. Begin by reading and making observations about Habakkuk 1:2–3.

Underline the words "how long shall I cry for help?" What can we assume based on this statement?

Based on these two verses, what are some of the things the prophet is seeing in Judah?

Today, we're going to go back a few years to examine some of the things that Habakkuk would have witnessed. Though not all scholars agree, many believe that Habakkuk would have begun his ministry to Judah sometime during King Josiah's final years and then wrote his message during the reign of his son, Jehoiakim.

THE DEATH OF KING JOSIAH

Read 2 Kings 22:1–2 and summarize Josiah's reign below.

In the history of the Jews, it is rare to find a king who obeyed God completely. Josiah was only eight years old when he began to reign, so was likely guided by godly influences for the beginning of his rule. By the time he was twenty-six, he decided to repair the temple of God. During the repairs, something was discovered that had been long forgotten.

Summarize 2 Kings 22:3–13 below. What was discovered? How did Josiah respond?

It's believed that Josiah heard the words of either Deuteronomy or Jeremiah, but most likely the former. With just one reading of God's Word, his heart was broken. He tore his robes in despair when he realized that the nation was not obeying God.

So many people today own Bibles, but they are unaffected when they read them. Every time we crack ours open, it should cause us to take immediate action to reform our lives.

Read James 1:22–25. What does it say we do to ourselves when we do not take action after reading God's Word?

What does the same verse say is the result of responding to it with intent?

Let's examine the two important things that Josiah did to bring the nation back into alignment with God's Word.

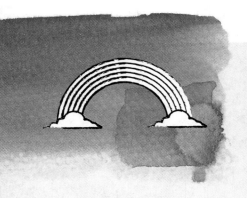

Welcome to your first rainbow! This study will help us grow in our understanding of *covenant*. Each time we come to one, you'll see the rainbow symbol. (That's the sign God gave to Noah when they made a covenant together.) When you are working within this shaded background, look at everything you read and write through the lens of our God's covenant promises.

COVENANT
(kev•nent)

noun. A usually formal, solemn, and binding agreement.[13]

Habakkuk references this concept a lot in his writing and many of the passages we will look at also reference it, including this one.

Read 2 Kings 23:1–3. What was the first thing Josiah did to reform Israel?

Much like a couple who'd gone through faithless times might renew their vows, God's people needed a do-over. And Josiah led them to formalize their love relationship. To remember their partnership.

Now, read 2 Kings 23:4–25 and summarize the second important reform action.

In the chart below, list some of the pagan gods and goddesses whose altars Josiah removed from the land of Judah. Then describe how it was worshipped.

NAME OF IDOL	HOW IT WAS WORSHIPPED

Baal, the primary god of the region, was demanding but generally appeased by animal sacrifice. At times of crisis, though, he required children. The Bible called that practice "detestable" (Deut. 12:31; 18:9–10).

Asherah preferred to be worshipped through ritual sex. This resulted in temple prostitution and rampant sexual sin.

Molech required child sacrifice. Remains of teeth and skeletons in archeological sites in Carthage demonstrate that infants of a specific age range—under three months old—were most commonly cremated in ritualistic ceremony.[14]

In addition to these deities, the people were turning to witches and mediums instead of God's prophets for help in making decisions and power to overcome evil.

These are just a few of the horrific things that had weaseled their way into holy spaces. No wonder Habakkuk was grieved and troubled.

It doesn't take an idol these days to make people act like pagans. How do you see these sins in your own nation today?

The good news is that Josiah's reforms caused the nation to begin to turn back to the One True God. But I'm afraid it didn't last long.

Read 2 Kings 23:29 and describe what happened to Josiah when he was thirty-nine years old. Why might this be a part of what burdened Habakkuk?

THE REIGN OF KING JEHOIAKIM

Read 2 Kings 23:31–37. Who ultimately replaced King Josiah and what kind of king was he?

TIME FOR TIMELINES!
Turn to pages 222–223 in the back of the book.

Find 609 BC on the timeline. Write: "Good King Josiah Dies."[15]

At the same spot on the timeline, write: "Evil King Jehoiakim Reigns."[16]

Habakkuk will speak for God during the reign of an evil king. The scene is set and it's horrific. Let the prostitutes loose and they don't have to be relegated to seedy alleys and secret places. Bring them back into the temple! Cue the priests who will happily help you burn your babies alive. (I could barely bring myself to type that.) And call for the spiritists and mediums so the people have a sense that they have some power to turn to, but it'll be the enslaving power of Satan that's luring them in. And God seems to have nothing to say about it.

It's hard for us to imagine how this was personal for Habakkuk. But no doubt, it was. Was he married? Did his wife go to the high places, much to his chagrin? Did he have a niece who was offered as a temple prostitute? Who else that he knew was killed in battle? Did he have a neighbor who'd sacrificed his baby in the name of Molech?

His eyes were burning with sights he could not unsee.

Does all of this weigh heavy on your heart? If you feel sad or sickened right now, be encouraged. That is evidence of the beauty of your heart, and it may be God beginning to speak to you. That makes it a good time to stop and speak to Him. In fact, any time our emotions are troubled, we should bring them to the One who can soothe them. Let's do that now.

What is it that you wish you could unsee? Have you been asking, *Why, God?* For how long? Write a poetic prayer to God that brings to Him all the suffering you see around you. Ask Him to bring healing to your heart and answers to your mind.

_____

_____

_____

_____

_____

_____

_____

MEDITATION 5

Wrestling with God

Your emotions are good.

God created them. And He declared that everything that He created is good (Gen. 1). The usefulness of them is this: they are messengers from God telling us to respond to something. If you are stressed out, it might be because you have taken on too much. Recalibrating will release the messenger from nagging you. Its job is done.

When we hit the storms of our life, it is natural for anxiety and stress, sadness and grief to bring messages to us. Ultimately, each message requires us to slow down and talk to God about the problems we see and how they are making us feel. If you do this, you will remain in control of how your emotions come and go.

But if you simply succumb to them without remembering the God who made them in the first place, they will get the upper hand and begin to define your life. The longer they linger, the greater your spiritual amnesia.

Today we'll discover Habakkuk's first habit and learn how it helped him talk to God about his fear.

Begin today's study activity by reading and making observations about Habakkuk 1:4.

Circle the word law in Habakkuk 1:4. Based on our study of 2 Kings 22:11–13, what specific law is this likely referring to?

Most of us have Bibles. I have so many that I probably cannot count them easily, but in my office right now I can see five.

When Habakkuk was alive, the Bible had not yet been collected into one volume, and very few people had read it. When Josiah was king, the Book of the Law was discovered. Some scholars believe it was all or a large part of the book of Deuteronomy.[17] No one even remembered it was there to be read. This led the good king to collect, identify, document, and begin placement of the Old Testament into a collective canon. He decreed that all of Judah should live in full compliance with the Law of God.

Look up the following verses and describe the practical use of God's Law.

Exodus 18:16

Exodus 18:20

Isaiah 1:17

Isaiah 2:3

Micah 6:8

Zechariah 7:9

By the time Habakkuk writes his book, King Jehoiakim has effectively discarded the law of God once again. The language the prophet uses in Habakkuk 1:4 to accuse God concerning the impotence of His law is bold!

What words does he use?

Remember the meaning of Habakkuk's name? Is he wrestling with God or embracing Him with these questions? Why do you think that?

Is that okay? Why or why not?

It's natural to veer toward one of two patterns in our communication with God when we are frustrated.

Some people perform for God and everyone else. They never question Him. Is that really an honest spiritual experience? Is their conforming behavior authentic? Doesn't this kind of communication sometimes produce legalism?

Others excel at expressing their opinions, questioning God as a norm. Aren't they rejecting truth? Isn't their behavior conforming to the god of their emotions? Doesn't this kind of living sometimes provide a license to sin?

The problem with these polar opposites is that they nullify grace. Check out this continuum for a better option: wrestling with God.

PERFORMING	WRESTLING	EXPRESSING
"I'll never question God."	*"I'll speak honestly. I'll listen bravely."*	*"I'll think/say whatever I want."*
Conformed Behavior	*Authentic, Whole Behavior*	*Emotion-based Behavior*
Dishonest	*Honestly Embraces Truth*	*Rejection of Truth*
PRODUCES LEGALISM	**PRODUCES FAITH**	**PRODUCES LICENSE**

Under each column above, write in an honest example of how you have been guilty of performing or expressing.

Now, in the middle column communicate how you wish you had chosen to live out one or both of those scenarios.

The practice of honest wrestling with God, especially in difficult times when He seems silent, is not in contrast to your faith. Rather, it has proven to be an authentic habit of the righteous who *live in faith*.

Read these passages. Write the name of the person who was verbally wrestling with God and why. Note how God revealed Himself to each of them.

Exodus 33:1–5, 12–23

1 Kings 19:9–14

Luke 7:18–23

When we show up to God with our questions and our doubts, He often reveals Himself to us too. When He does, our faith is bolstered.

HOW TO SQUEEZE FAITH OUT OF DOUBT

This is going to seem really basic, but indulge me. To whom is Habakkuk speaking in the passage we're studying today?

When the prophet witnesses horrible sexual sin, tragic murder of babies, witchcraft, and idolatry, he does not tweet about it, lobby against his government, or stand on the street corners with signs of God's judgment. When he sees his friends and family deeply impacted by all the corruption, he doesn't write a blog, post his political position, gossip with friends, or withdraw and feel sorry for himself. He talks to God about his burden.

What does this say to your heart?

Read Romans 10:17. Why do you think talking to God has the potential to produce faith in your heart when you're struggling with His silence and doubting His work in this world?

The Six Habits of Living by Faith

Turn to page 224 at the back of your book. You'll find the six practices or habits of living by faith that Habakkuk demonstrated. They will help you know how to respond to God when He seems silent or you face suffering. Study that right now.

Here is the first of the six habits. Circle key words that will help you remember the action you need to take for this first habit.

1. Remember to wrestle with God when He seems silent.

Habakkuk isn't just a wrestler. He's a heavyweight champion.

Have you spoken honestly with God? Or are you bringing a guarded version of your heart to Him? Maybe you're not being honest because you don't take time to hear His opinion because you're so busy obsessing over yours.

Try to find the truth-filled place of honest wrestling today.

Make a decision to begin to wrestle honestly with God about what frustrates you. A good thing to talk to Him about is whether you're talking to Him about your frustrations or just telling others about them. Only He can fix what's wrong. That does not mean you can't express your doubts to godly people who can help you wrestle with them. But it generally excludes us from the noisy public clamor on social media and other public forums where we aren't in safe places to hear from the Lord. Prayerfully process this in a written letter to God below.

It's the end of the first week. That means it's time to muscle up on the meditation as you consider what God's Spirit needs you to do with what you've experienced. Prayerfully skim this week's meditation assignments. Ask God's Spirit to direct your mind to anything He knows to be important for you. Then, write responses to these two statements below.

• *Ask God to identify a Bible verse or sentence that He is prompting you to embrace and understand.*

• *Reword that Bible verse or sentence into a prayer. Ask God what He wants you to do with it. Write a response to Him about what you sense Him saying. Determine in your heart to live it out this week.*

❧ ❧ ❧

Why Does God Seem Silent?

WE ARE ALL IN _____.

The Babylonian _____ is a picture of something _____. We're all _____ to feel like we are _____.

THERE'S A MESSAGE IN THE SILENCE

5 CHARACTERISTICS OF GOD'S VOICE

1. He often says something that's _____ to my _____, but is never _____ to His (Isa. 55:8, 9; Num. 23:19).

2. He _____ my _____ (John 16:8).

3. He speaks to me more _____ when I am _____ (1 John 2:3–6; Isa. 59:2).

4. He tells me things I _____ (John 14:26).

5. There is _____ to His voice (Ps. 29:3; Rev. 14:2; Ex. 19:19; Job 40:9).

Habit #2: Remember to look and see where God is at work.

Answers to the podcast fill-in-the-blanks can be found on page 215.

WEEK 2

Remember to Look for God's Work

"Please help me! Please don't send me back," cried the little girl who'd fled the Hindu temple in the middle of the night.[1]

The girl would be beaten, or perhaps even killed, if she was taken back to the temple where she served as a *Devadasi*.[2] Girls as young as five held the title. Parents brought them willingly, turning a blind eye to the raucous sexual appetites of those awaiting the girls.

Keeping seven-year-old Preena meant Amy Carmichael could be charged with kidnapping and sentenced to prison.

But how could she turn her away? Maybe this was why God had led her to India in the first place.

Amy had every reason to stay home. To never leave Ireland. A debilitating battle with neuroglia, ranked as one of the most excruciating types of pain on the McGill Pain index, sometimes caused her to collapse. It would take weeks in bed to recover when she had a flare-up.

But the nations called to her.

She had frequent physical setbacks in her quest to find the home of her heart. England. Japan. Sri Lanka. The climates agitated her nerves, sending her home again and again to recuperate.

Others would have given up, but Amy had a unique perspective on trials.

"Let us not be surprised when we have to face difficulties. When the wind blows hard on a tree, the roots stretch and grow the stronger. Let it be so with us. Let us not be weaklings, yielding to every wind that blows, but strong in spirit to resist."[3]

The wind blew her to where her health would benefit from the sunshine: India.

It was there that she became one of the world's human trafficking opponents. And a fearless one at that.

Amy would become *Amma*, or mother, to hundreds of Indian girls during her fifty-three years in India.

Would she have gone there if it were not for the pain?

Maybe God was at work, even in that.

MEDITATION 1

Changing the way you see

The Bible is not about me.

That probably does not surprise you.

But it's also not about you, and that might come as a bit of a shock.

Think about it.

I have a tendency to read the Scriptures from my own personal perspective. I pick out a psalm when I want to seek comfort. A proverb comes in handy if I need a bit of practical living advice. The Sermon on the Mount is great for feeling "blessed." If left to my own devices, I pick and choose what I read and apply.

But the Bible is not about us. It's about the whole world.

While it is true that a central theme of the Scriptures is our personal relationship with God, there is a broader picture that most of us are missing in our self-absorbed approach. The Bible places our personal story into a larger rescue plan: the salvation of all of humanity.

And, oh, do we need saving.

I woke up to these headlines today:

- *Why are young Americans killing themselves?*[4]
- *Iran OKs bill calling US military, Pentagon terrorists after Qasem Soleimani killing.*[5]
- *Another powerful quake jolts Puerto Rico.*[6]
- *Indian steelmaker ArcelorMittal accused of manipulating tests after toxic spill killed thousands of fish.*[7]

Self-hatred. Nationalism at all costs. A quaking earth. Anything for a buck. These are not new problems. They are not singular problems. They are the long scream of The Fall. And that is a problem that God is working to solve even now. As He does, He solves all of your problems too.

Of course, looking at the Bible through this lens of global concern may feel about as natural to you and me as a pair of new prescription contacts. But let's try it on this week anyway. I hear if you keep the contacts in, you'll not only get used to them, but they'll change the way you see.

Read and make observations about Habakkuk 1:5. We will focus on just the first half of this important verse today.

Let's quickly review what we studied last week. Habakkuk complains to God about the hideous behavior of his nation, Judah. He accuses God of being silent in the face of rampant sexual sin, horrific human sacrifice, sorcery, and really bad leadership. The prophet cries out with two questions:

- "How long 'til you do something?"
- "Why does evil exist in this world?"

After Habakkuk brings these two complaints to God, the seemingly Silent One speaks up.

In Habakkuk 1:5, God uses four action words (verbs) which tell the prophet what He wants him to do. What are they?

Compare verse 5 with verse 3 in Habakkuk 1. Circle the two pairs of words you see.

God answers Habakkuk using the same words the prophet did to present his complaint. He throws them right back at the prophet. God says: *Let me tell you where you should be looking and what I need you to see.*

Where does God instruct him to focus his vision?

Essentially, God's saying: *I heard you. I know you're looking at and seeing your own problems. But I want you to look at and see the nations.*

LOOK AND SEE THE NATIONS

Check out this map of the ancient Middle East as it would have looked during Habakkuk's life.

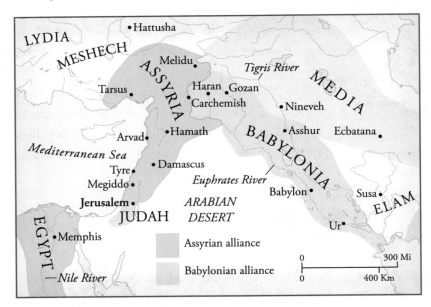

THE SETTING OF HABAKKUK

Identify the four significant nations in Habakkuk's ancient world. Write them below.

Which two nations seem to be world powers based on size?

Today I want us to begin to understand why God wanted Habakkuk to look and see the nations. We'll do that by examining Assyria—the world superpower at the time.

THE HANGING GARDEN OF . . . NINEVEH?

According to many historians, the Neo-Assyrian Empire (912–612 BC) was the first true domain of the world. To be such a power, you had to have a king or a queen. Check. You had to hold multiple countries or states under your supreme control. Check. And that meant the Mark Zuckerburgs of the era could make a few million *mina* and also make a mark. Check. Check.

The wealthy made their mark by building stuff. Nineveh, the great capital of the empire, had a massive defensive wall with fifteen gates, aqueducts and irrigation ditches and public places, a palace with eighty rooms, and a lot of parks and gardens. There is even sufficient argument that one of the seven wonders of the ancient world—The Hanging Gardens of Babylon—were actually The Hanging Gardens of Nineveh.[8] You might think of Nineveh as an ancient New York City, full of culture and class, worthy of being on every ancient traveler's vacation plan.

Spoiler alert: this nation loses in the chess game of the nations. That's significant. It would have been as shocking to imagine as New York City falling into the Atlantic Ocean tomorrow. So, let's land here and see what we can glean. We'll use the book of Jonah to learn a bit more about God's heart concerning the nations.

TIME FOR TIMELINES!
Turn to pages 222–223 in the back of the book.

Find 755 BC on the timeline. Write: "Jonah Goes to Nineveh."[9]

About 150 years before Habakkuk begins his ministry, Jonah is serving as a prophet for the Northern Kingdom (Israel). The book of the Bible bearing his name is the only prophetic book that tells the story of a prophet rather than recording a message from him.

Read Jonah 1:1–2. Why does God send Jonah to Nineveh? How does God describe the people and city?

Jonah has ideas of his own. He doesn't want to take God's message to Nineveh.

Read 2 Kings 19:17 and take a guess at why Jonah didn't want to obey God.

The Assyrian Empire may have been a site for ancient tourists to see, but the polytheistic people were ruthlessly driven by selfish ambition and greed. The warriors were cruel and reveled in the art that displayed their handiwork. Ancient scenes of soldiers ripping the tongues from captives, flaying their enemies alive, beheading opposing leaders, and forcing prisoners of war to grind up the bones of their fallen comrades adorn the British Museum's recreation of Assyrian art.[10]

Historian Simon Anglim writes that "though the Assyrian armies were respected and feared . . . they were most of all hated."[11]

Jonah cannot imagine why God would want to warn these barbarians. If judgment was actually coming, it would be well-deserved. The prophet sets sail in the opposite direction with some soft-hearted sailors.

Running from God never works. And it did not for Jonah. God chased him with the wind. Jonah tells the sailors that his God is mad at him and promises that if they throw him overboard, the storm will stop. They do it and a big fish swallows him and three days later spits him out.

God tells the soggy prophet the same thing He'd told him before: *Go to Nineveh!*

In spite of sharing the local disdain for Nineveh, Jonah cries "uncle." He gets himself to the capital of the Assyrian Empire, but his attitude smells about as bad as the inside of that big fish. In Hebrew, he delivers an epic five-word sermon. *Five words!* He certainly does not wax eloquent. No mention of what Nineveh has done wrong or how to make it right. Not even a mention of God. He delivers the minimal amount of information. Even so, the presence of God is so thick on this reluctant minister that the whole city—including its cows—repents! So, God does not destroy them.

All's well that ends well, right? Not exactly. Jonah is ticked.

Read Jonah 4:1–11. Focus in on verses 1–3. Why is Jonah angry?

What a bummer! Poor Jonah actually serves a merciful God full of compassion. (He wasn't complaining about that when the fish spat him out, was he?) In fact, Yahweh is so compassionate that He grows a leafy plant to shelter the worn-out prophet while he recovers from his ordeal. Jonah sure is a plant lover, but he has no green thumb. His vine dies. And he is sad. And, maybe a bit embarrassed. After all, the way the story panned out sort of discredited him.

Summarize what God communicates in Jonah 4:9–11. What questions did He ask the prophet? How many people did God spare that day?

The gentle confrontation God presents to Jonah is a little bit like the one we see referenced in Habakkuk 1:5. God essentially says: *Jonah, you're sad about your leafy plant! Isn't it okay that I feel sorry for all the people of Nineveh who lost their way? And the cows too?*

God invited Jonah to get over himself. Perhaps the very reason he was chosen for the assignment was so he could see the need of the whole world.

Habakkuk gets a similar invitation from God when he's invited to look at the nations.

Could God have such a call for you?

In the original Hebrew language, the word "look" in Habakkuk 1:5 was plural. God was not just talking to the prophet, but to everyone who would hear the message. He was saying, "Everybody, look at the nations!" (Or as my friend, Nancy DeMoss Wolgemuth, said when she was teaching on Habakkuk: God was saying, "ya'll look!")[12]

God wants *you* to look and see the nations.

Read the verses below from the New Testament and summarize how they communicate God's desire for the nations today.

2 Peter 3:9

Matthew 28:19

Mark 16:15

Revelation 7:9

Summarize what you sense God's Word telling you about His heart for the nations.

Are you focused on your own needs, the needs of your community, family, or nation without any regard to how your story fits into God's big picture story of rescuing the entire world? God invites you and me to "get over" ourselves.

He's calling us to "look and see" the nations.

Do you have a love for the nations or a specific foreign nation? Perhaps you desire to be a missionary or an ambassador, a travel agent or an international businesswoman. Or maybe you are like some of the women I know who report having experienced a longing or love for another country as a little girl. If you consume international news with a heart that breaks, it might be God inviting you to "look" and "see." Have you ever experienced those things? Even if you just have a good case of wanderlust, is it possible there's more to it than a desire to see the sights? Write a prayer to God processing through *any* ways in which He has planted in you a desire to look and see the nations.

MEDITATION 2

Looking and seeing

Hannah had trouble that made her tremble.

How long had she prayed for a baby? We don't know. What we do know is that on this day she has come to register her complaint with God in the temple.

If wrestling in prayer were a competition, this woman would win every match. Eli the priest has never seen the likes of it. He accuses her: *Are you drunk?*

No, not drunk. Just whacked out with worry and filled up with frustration.

Hannah tells Eli, "I am a woman troubled in spirit. I have drunk neither wine nor strong drink, but I have been pouring out my soul before the LORD" (1 Sam. 1:15). The word translated as *pouring out* is the Hebrew verb *sapak,* which means "to shed, to spill, to be scattered."[13] Sounds like messy business to me. This is not your neat and clean prayer list, but a spilling of a broken soul with no sense of where or when things might land.

It was honest.

Her vision is hyper-focused on her barren womb.

God sees too.

But He also sees a barren nation.

Maybe it's just me, but these special contacts are hard to get used to. With one eye adjusting to the it's-not-all-about-me filter and the other fitted with the-Bible-is-actually-about-the-rescue-of-all-the-nations transition lens, I need a little time. I'm no drama queen, but I can't go on! I need to get used to the corrective lens prescribed yesterday by our Great Ophthalmologist.

For today's study activity, we'll slow down a bit to continue correcting the way we see. Put your finger in Habakkuk, but I also want you to open your Bible to 1 Samuel 3:1–20. Begin by reading the passage and make any notes on your observations. Look closely at the first verse.

Circle the word in the New Living Translation version of Habakkuk 1:1 that also appears in 1 Samuel 3:1.

> This is the message that the prophet Habakkuk received in a vision.
> **HAB. 1:1 (NLT)**

I hope this word sounds familiar to you. We studied it during Meditation 3 last week.

Turn to page 30 if you need help, but try to recall the Hebrew word that is translated into the English word vision.

Let's dig a little deeper into that word. We'll peek into the life of Samuel, the baby Hannah wanted so badly. The once-barren woman promised God that she'd give her baby back to Him, and she has made good on that. Samuel is now living with Eli the priest though he is still just a boy. But God is about to do something.

Read 1 Samuel 3:1–21, where you'll notice the word hazon *makes an important appearance. Answer these questions.*

What was true about visions in those days?

How does God choose to bring revelation to the nation?

Since God brought hazon *through this boy, what does that make him?*

Why do you think it was confusing for Samuel at first?

Find the verse that sounds a lot like Habakkuk 1:5. What sounds similar?

What does verse 19 say Samuel did with the words God gave him? And what do you think that meant?

Let's fast-forward a few years to when Samuel is a grown man. Saul is the first king of Israel and suffering from a bad case of jealousy for his soon-to-be successor, David. He's so blinded by it that he tries to kill the shepherd boy. It is right after one of these attempts that we pick up the story.

Read 1 Samuel 19:18–24. Is Samuel still the only one hearing God's voice?

Who does this passage reveal has received hazon*?*

Some Bible scholars believe that this passage refers to a school of prophecy that was birthed during the years of Samuel's ministry. Habakkuk may have attended this very school.[14] Imagine that! Way back when the first king of Israel was messing things up, God began to solve the problem Habakkuk would see during his lifetime by establishing a way to train prophets to recognize His voice.

God does not just work to solve the problems of the whole world, but to solve them *for all of time*. He cares about the history of His world.

He used the baby Hannah begged for to break a revelation drought in Israel and then used that boy to train others to listen for and hear God's voice. Hundreds of years later, Habakkuk was one of many who was still recognizing *hazon*.

And it all began with one woman's troubles.

Hannah was a woman whose heart had a personal burden. God saw her. He saw her desires. What did she want? Write it in the blank below.

Hannah wanted a _____.

God also saw the condition of His people. He had a national burden. The country He'd nurtured and loved was like an unfaithful spouse, breaking His heart and testing His authority. What did He need? Write it in the blank below.

God needed a _____.

Sometimes the purpose of the waiting is to give our hearts time to want to be a part of God's plan.

Read 1 Samuel 1:11. What vow does Hannah present to God? And how is that significant in light of the fact that she's probably been begging God to have a baby for a long time?

Who knows? Maybe God was just waiting for her to say "yes" to His request so He could say "yes" to hers. He needed someone to have the ears to hear Him. Baby Samuel would be the one. That, my friend, is nothing short of an amazing plan.

I wonder if Hannah marveled at what God was up to when she was an old woman and saw God move mightily through her son? Did it thrill her to see that God used her personal pain to poise a nation to hear His voice?

GOD STILL SPEAKS

In the Old Testament, God spoke to His people through prophets. He also spoke through dreams, signs and wonders, whispers, and other ways. Once He even used a stubborn donkey. But is He still speaking today?

Look up these verses and record what each teaches us about hearing God's voice.

John 10:27

Mark 13:11; Matthew 10:20; Luke 12:12; John 14:26

Luke 11:28

John 8:31, 32

John 8:37–38

I believe God still speaks to us today. And I believe He wants to speak to you. Today we hear Him through the Bible, circumstances, and wise advisors. All of these are rooted in recognizing the voice of our sweet Holy Spirit.

I hope this week's podcast helped you to learn how to recognize His voice. If you have not already listened to it, be sure to do so. In it, I share five characteristics of God's voice. If you have already heard the content, reference your notes at the beginning of this week to answer the question below.

What are some of the characteristics of God's voice that you have experienced? List each, and then write about when and how.

What qualities would you like to grow to experience?

Be patient with yourself. It can take some time to begin to recognize what His voice feels like and how it sounds. But your discernment will grow as you spend more time with Him. And as you recognize it, you will be amazed, and you will see how He is at work around you.

Today I am amazed. God has spoken to me again to show me something I've wondered about for quite some time. He's revealed something to me that I did not see in real time. Tears are welling up in my eyes at the newness of clear vision.

I was fifteen when my life was altered by a season of sin. Thrown off course with a diagnosable case of amnesia, I got lost in my lust. Then, shrouded in my shame. What a work it took for God to rescue me! It seemed to take Him years to show up. *But that wasn't true at all.*

You see, my mother has long prayed Habakkuk 1:5 over my life. I never knew when she began. Until now. She was looking back through an old Bible and found the first time she lifted those words on my behalf. They were marked with a date. The years can be counted. I do the math on my fingers. Stop dead when I find the answer. Tears flow. Praises rise.

I was fifteen.

He was at work all along. And not just to set me free, but to make me a mouthpiece of His forgiveness and healing. When I finally stabilized, God birthed a ministry through my story. Hundreds of thousands have read my testimony in book form. It amazes me that He would use this poster child for sin to speak His Truth to a generation embroiled in sexual confusion.

God is always at work, even when He seems silent.

The Six Habits of Living by Faith

Turn to the back of your book. You'll find the six practices or habits of living by faith that Habakkuk demonstrated. Review that list again.

Here are habits number one and two. Circle key words that will help you remember the action you need to take for each of them.

1. Remember to wrestle with God when He seems silent.

2. Remember to look to see where God is at work.

Write the key words or phrases of the first and second habit on the following lines.

_____

_____

Maybe, like Samuel in Israel or Habakkuk in Judah, you've had a drought of hearing God's voice. I pray He uses our time in the pages of Habakkuk to let His words fall in a mighty downpour so you can begin to see where He is working.

Have you ever considered that the burden you are currently facing could be used by God in the big picture plan He has for this world? Maybe He's been prompting you through the still small voice through prayer, circumstances, or other people. Maybe you've been hearing His voice but didn't recognize it. Write below anything you believe God may be trying to say to you about your current trial and the future He has planned for you. How might He have His eye on a bigger picture as He works in your life? Don't be afraid of getting it wrong, but trust that He will confirm or redirect you.

MEDITATION 3

Sometimes there's a message in the silence

Children have certainly said some funny things when they misunderstand the Bible.

"Lot's wife was a pillar of salt by day, but a ball of fire by night."[15]
"The first commandment was when Eve told Adam to eat the apple."[16]

"When you get scared, God will bring you your quilt. He said the Comforter would come."[17]

From the mouths of babes!

I wonder if God ever laughs at the way adults misinterpret the Bible. Have you ever noticed how often promises from Scripture are taken out of context?

For example, some people say "I can do all things through Christ" when they need a pep talk to meet a deadline, pay their bills, or pass a test. But Paul wasn't doing much when he penned that verse. He was in prison and the point of what he wrote was contentment, not attainment.

When we isolate one Bible verse from those that surround it, we often miss the true message God is sending to us.

The verse from Habakkuk that we'll study today is an often misused promise of God.

> Look among the nations, and see;
>   wonder and be astounded.
> For I am doing a work in your days
>   that you would not believe if told.
> **(HAB. 1:5)**

It has been plastered all over Pinterest and printed on a t-shirt or two. We love to claim the promise that God is working to do something so wonderful that we could barely comprehend it. (There we go again, making the Bible all about us!)

Today, we will look closely at this verse and come to fully understand what's being communicated. It won't take long to see the prophet is heading into a scenario that looks a whole lot like the Middle East of today. (What we are witnessing in that part of the globe is one of the world's most enduring conflicts.) Habakkuk's about to be told there are some upcoming battles that don't go so well for his nation. Exactly what is it that he won't believe even if he were told? *Just how bad it's going to get?!*

I bet that inspired you to study today! Nevertheless, God's Word has good treasures for you and me, so let's dig in.

Read and make observations about Habakkuk 1:5 once again. We're focusing on the second part of the verse today.

Habakkuk was not the first Hebrew to cry out to God with this question: *do you see us?* And this wasn't the first time God's people needed some good solid deliverance. Today I want to travel back in time to consider one of the nations Habakkuk probably had his eye on when God told him to "look" and "see."

Look up Exodus 2:23–25 and answer these questions.

Who was crying out to God?

From what nation?

Why were they asking God to see them?

What was God doing?

Long before the nation of Judah had adopted the customs and behaviors of Nineveh, the people of God had adopted the customs and behaviors of Egypt. In doing so, they'd forgotten God.

It's hard to worship and obey someone you can't remember.

Look up Deuteronomy 8:5. How does God describe His response to the bad behavior of His people?

Maybe the purpose of the Egyptian slavery and all those plagues wasn't just to set His people free. Is it possible we take even that out of context?

THE PURPOSE OF THE EGYPTIAN PLAGUES

When God shows up to deliver His people from Egyptian slavery, Pharaoh is reluctant to release his pyramid-building workforce. The Bible records that God sent ten plagues to move their conversation along. Let's consider the purposes of them. If the only purpose was to set the Israelites free, wouldn't one cataclysmic event have been sufficient?

Look up the following verses. Record what God called the plagues. If there is any reference to "who God is" or "the gods of Egypt", make a note of it.

Exodus 7:3–5

Exodus 8:22, 23

Exodus 10:1, 2

Exodus 12:12

A significant purpose of the plagues may have been to remind the world who God is and to execute judgment on the many false gods worshipped in the polytheistic ancient world.[18] They were signs of His power. Over what?

Skim Exodus 7:14–11:10 and list the ten plagues below.

SIGN NUMBER	TYPE OF PLAGUE POSSIBLE	CORRESPONDING "GOD"
Sign #1		
Sign #2		
Sign #3		
Sign #4		
Sign #5		
Sign #6		

Sign #7		
Sign #8		
Sign #9		
Sign #10		

Using this chart of Egyptian gods, match them to any corresponding signs or plagues. Place them on the previous chart.

RA	god of the sun; named after the first Pharaoh
NEPHTHYS	the river goddess
BES	god of dwarves, protector of households, mother, and children; had the power to scare off evil spirits
HEQET	goddess of fertility, water, and renewal; had the head of a frog
ISIS	goddess of magic and medicine; wife of Ra
SEKHMET, SERAPIS, IMHOTE	gods of healing
UATCHIT	god of the flies
SERAPIA	goddess of the locusts
PTAH, MNEVIS, HATHOR, AMNON	gods associated with bulls and cows
SETH	god of storms and disorder
HATHOR	goddess of love and protection; had the head of a cow
PHARAOH	considered the ultimate power over Egypt; many of the gods were eventually named after them

Each of the plagues confronted and overpowered things that the Egyptians considered powerful, and therefore worshipped.

Read Joshua 24:14. What does it tell us God's people were doing when they lived in Egypt?

The miraculous plagues were, in part, to reveal God to Egypt and the surrounding nations. And to His people. They were not just meant for the deliverance of Israel. They also jogged the memory of a people that had forgotten the One True God.

God saw the Israelites during their time of slavery in Egypt and desired to deliver them from slavery. And from themselves.

Read 2 Kings 23:29–34 again. Record what it tells us about Judah's relationship with Egypt in the days of Habakkuk.

TIME FOR TIMELINES!
Turn to pages 222–223 in the back of the book.

Find 605 BC on the timeline. (What an eventful year!) Write: "Judah becomes a vassal nation for Egypt."[19]

Spiritual amnesia does not only make us forget who God is, but we forget what He's rescued us from. Why is it that the same old bondage seems to welcome us back again and again? Unless we remain vigilant, old enslavements will become new alliances.

I believe that for Israel and Judah, there was a message in the silence. God is making space for them to feel the separation of their sin. He wanted them to turn away from their idols and turn back to Him.

What's this have to do with you and me? By examining God's responses to His people throughout history, we can determine His character and how He may be seeing us today.

Is there a message in the silence you may be experiencing?

IS THERE A MESSAGE IN GOD'S SILENCE?

When we are in a love relationship with God, He speaks to us. I'm able to hear God's voice more readily when I'm obedient (1 John 2:3–6; Isa. 59:2). When we obey God, we prove that we love Him.

On the other hand, I am able to hear Him less when there is sin in my life. Sin separates us from God. When our love relationship is broken by disobedience or unconfessed sin, it is like the Wi-Fi is weak. We cannot hear Him.

UNTIL WE MAKE OUR HEARTS RIGHT BEFORE GOD, WE WILL BE UNABLE TO HEAR HIS VOICE CLEARLY. SOMETIMES THAT IS THE MESSAGE IN THE SILENCE.

Do you think God sees any evidence in your life that you've forgotten who He is? That you've been seduced by the gods of this world like materialism, power, sex, or worldly beauty? Or that old enslavements to sin are sneaking in on you?

Here's the good news: Habakkuk 1:5 was written to God's people when they needed Him because they'd acted like—to best translate—heathens. Your sin does not negate God's work in your life. Rather, it is one of the reasons that His love compels Him to be at work on your behalf. Will there be consequences? Possibly. But does He intend to rescue you? Absolutely!

Look up Hebrews 12:6. What does it tell you about how God feels when He has to discipline us?

God sees you. And He hears you. Difficult times do not mean that He does not have compassion. He loves you. If the difficult time you are facing is discipline, His silence does not equal inaction. Right now, God may be looking upon you and your circumstances with one hope: that you would be like Josiah and remember your faith and re-surrender your heart and life to Him so that He can get to the business of your rescue.

God's apparent silence is not always evidence that there is sin in your life. Sometimes, it's just evidence of our broken world. But it is always wise to examine your heart to see if there is anything between you and Him. Spend time today taking a full inventory of your heart. Confess anything that God brings to your mind. Write a prayer of repentance to God.

MEDITATION 4

God sees things differently

Do you ever make up plans for how God can lighten your load? Fix your failures? Payout on His promises? Shore up your success?

I do.

Sometimes I think maybe He just needs a good idea or two. So, I spend no small amount of time imagining how He might crown me once and for all Grand Controller of my little corner of the world.

That's not usually the way things turn out. God's answers to my prayers are often very different from the ones I expect.

You too?

Today we will discover a little twist in Habakkuk's story. He's about to fully comprehend what God was talking about when He used the word "amazed."

And he's not gonna like it one bit.

Begin today's study activity by reading and making observations about Habakkuk 1:6–8.

As we continue on with God's conversation with Habakkuk, we learn the first of two reasons why the prophet may be amazed. Let's examine God's answer to Habakkuk's complaints.

It's safe to assume that the prophet was expecting God would deliver a word of judgment, but the befuddled man hears one he just cannot imagine. First, the nation is going to fall into the hands of a pagan ruler who will take captives. And second, the people group God says will overtake Judah don't seem powerful enough to get the job done.

Answer these questions about the people group God is going to use to discipline His own children.

Who were they? What words does God use to describe them?

How far would their power extend?

How would Judah and other nations feel about them?

Double underline the words "I am raising up" in Habakkuk 1:6. Who was choosing the birth of this new superpower?

When God spoke those words, Habakkuk's jaw had to have dropped down to his knocking knees. What God was saying would surely have been hard to believe. Let's look at some maps to figure out why.

Look back on page 50 at our map of the ancient Middle East in the time of our prophet.

Can you find Chaldea?
Me either. Because it barely existed! Look again. Let me show you where you'd find the Chaldeans.

See that itty-bitty little city named Ur? Write CHALDEA beside it.

This is where the nation *used* to exist. At the time Habakkuk was hearing God's plan, there were just a few of them left and the nation had been absorbed by another.

Look at the map to figure out who had overtaken Chaldea, and write the name of that nation below.

Maybe you didn't need to look at a map to figure that one out, because some translations of the Bible skip over this little fact about the Chaldeans being used to judge Judah. Those versions just report that the Babylonians would be God's tool of judgment. That's too bad. They're missing just how shocking this news would have been to Habakkuk.

The God of Judah was pregnant with a plan to put His children in time-out. He was raising up the Chaldeans to discipline the nation of Judah by taking them into captivity. Why?

Even though we looked at it yesterday, let's breathe it in once again. Circle the sole word that motivates God's discipline in the verse below.

For the Lord disciplines the one he loves,
    and chastises every son whom he receives.
(HEB. 12:6)

Today, I had to rescue my horses—Trigg and Truett. I awakened to find they'd busted through a fairly sturdy fence to exploit the hay leftovers my picky llamas leave behind daily. They risked life and limb to break through to it. When I found them, Trigg looked dead. I was terrified. It took a while for my heart to stop pumping double-time even after I verified that my paunchy palomino was only taking a glorious nap in the winter sunshine.

I had no choice. They had not obeyed the boundaries I put in place to keep them safe. They were banished from their own big pasture. I took them both straight to the barn and locked them in for the day.

Why did I execute judgment on my boys? I love them. And I want them to be around for a good long time.

Did I rescue them? Yes.

Did I punish them? Also, affirmative.

The themes of judgment and salvation run on two parallel tracks throughout scripture.

—NANCY DEMOSS WOLGEMUTH[20]

Generally, the reason we need saving is because we got ourselves into trouble to begin with. We often think of addictions to substances or unhealthy sex, self-harming or spending, over-eating or gambling as bondages that need to be broken. But we very rarely see the most deadly of dependencies: the worship of self. Prideful, self-centered thinking is always at the root of our sin. And sin inevitably leads to brokenness. No exceptions.

Look up Acts 13:40, 41 where the apostle Paul once again quotes our boy, Habakkuk. Answer the following questions.

What verse from Habakkuk is referenced here?

How does Paul use it?

Why do you think he says it could apply to them?

Paul warns his contemporaries that if they do what Judah did—fail to remember who God is and how to honor Him as the center of our lives—they could face the same kind of judgment as Judah. That warning is for us, too. Oh, how we must be careful . . . or before we know it, we will be in bondage to the enemy.

Satan does not take innocent people captive.
—JOHN PIPER[21]

And that brings us back to the news that the Chaldeans are about to carry Jewish captives off into bondage.

As we finish our study time today, imagine that one of the few Chaldeans in Babylon has been making a name for himself. Nabopolassar manages to climb his way to the top and secure a spot as the first Chaldean king of Babylon. He was not satisfied to rule Babylon as it was. He wanted more. So, he formed an alliance with the Medes to successfully confront the superpowers of Assyria and Egypt. It'll only be a short matter of time before Judah gets overtaken too. And guess what the ancient Middle East world map would look like then?

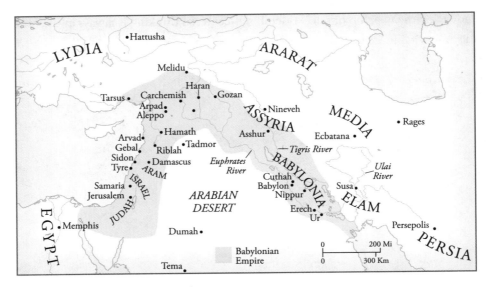

THE BABYLONIAN EMPIRE

Kind of gives you a whole new context for the "amazing" thing God is about to do, doesn't it?

Let's be women who study our Bible so well that we don't misrepresent God's promises.

Some of them aren't laden with happy news, but all of them are overflowing with useful news.

Hold these "amazing" thoughts. We'll come back to them in a few weeks.

For now, let's spend another day getting honest with God about what might cause distance and silence between us and Him.

Today's prayer activity involves getting honest about your self-centeredness. Notice, I did not say *if* you have any self-centeredness. It's a constant battle for most of us. Write a courageous prayer asking God to give you the ability to see your current life direction the way that He sees it. Confess to Him anything He shows you that is not guided by surrender to Him.

MEDITATION 5

The danger of friendly captivity

FAST FORWARD TO BABYLON >>>

To gain understanding concerning Habakkuk's prophecy, we will from time to time fast-forward to the book of Daniel where Judah is enduring the exile. Welcome to Babylon.

It gives me no small amount of joy every time I read about archeological discoveries verifying what we read in the pages of our Bibles. And the excavation site of Babylon supplies many wondrous confirmations.

Babylon's ruins lie in modern-day Iraq just fifty miles southwest of Baghdad. The city was excavated between 1899 and 1917 by a German team of archeologists. One of the fascinating finds is a collection of clay tablets named The Babylonian Chronicles. The one which summarizes the years 605–594 BC describes how the nation rose up against Jerusalem. The inscription con-

firms numerous details of the biblical account: the siege of Jerusalem, the exile of King Jehoiakim, and the stolen treasures. It even gives an exact date for the takeover: March 16, 596 BC.[22]

Amazing! But what's more amazing—that we can look *back* on these events through historical documentation, or that Habakkuk was able to look *forward* to them through supernatural inspiration?

Begin today's study activity by reading and making observations about Habakkuk 1:9, 11.

Answer these questions about the Chaldeans, who we will henceforth refer to as the Babylonians now that we have Nabopolassar's crown neatly placed on his royal head.

How does this passage say they will come when they arrive to take over Judah?

Circle the word "captives." Based on the poetic wording found here, how frequently do the Babylonians seem to carry off new exiles to their homeland?

How do they interact with the rulers of other nations?

How does this passage clearly reveal the self-absorbed mindset of Babylonia?

During Habakkuk's lifetime, King Nabopolassar's reign certainly left a mark on the ancient world, but it was short-lived. However, you might recognize the name of his son, the crown prince: **Nebuchadnezzar.** He was the longest reigning, most powerful monarch of the

Neo-Babylonian Empire. Under his leadership, the nation held its ground against Assyria and Egypt, eventually taking theirs.

TIME FOR TIMELINES!
Turn to pages 222–223 in the back of the book.

Find 605–538 BC on the timeline. Write: "Exiles Return Home."

Read Daniel 1:1–5 and answer the following questions.

When did Babylon take Judah?

Specifically, what city was the stage for the battle?

Who does this passage say ultimately had authority over the outcome?

What physical objects did Nebuchadnezzar take and why?

Which of the residents of Jerusalem did he want exiled to Babylon?

Fill in the spaces below with qualities the king of Babylon looked for when choosing someone to use to accomplish his work.

FAMILY BACKGROUND	PHYSICAL QUALITIES	INTELLECT & EDUCATION

For so many years, I was a captive. First, I was in bondage to my sin. When I found my way out of that prison cell, I just moved down the hall and accepted the invitation to live in the "shame" ward. When I noticed that door was also unlocked by my Jesus, I happily accepted the enemy's invitation into the "disqualified" cell.

How does that relate to Daniel and his friends? Through all of it, I believed the lie that I had very little to offer to the body of Christ, so it did not matter if I was a contributor or not. What did I have to offer? I embraced the complacence of cooperating with the enemy's plans.

I wonder if you have a hard time seeing all the great qualities God has planted in you. While it is true that these earthly traits listed in the first chapter of Daniel are not the most important things God plants in humanity, there's a parallel to be seen. Even when we cannot, the enemy sees how we are capable of influence.

The thought occurs to me: all of the captives had potential to be influencers and find themselves on the pages of Scripture. But only these four men refused to cooperate with the enemy. Most of them were renamed in Babylon.

RENAMED BY BABYLON

It seems the plan of Nebuchadnezzar was to bring all the influencers to his capital so he could indoctrinate them. Rather than the back-breaking slavery the Egyptians used to put the Israelites into bondage, Babylon would use education, opportunity, and good food as seduction. That doesn't sound like captivity. (It sounds like college.) It was what you might call *friendly captivity*. There's nothing more dangerous! The king of Babylon sought to keep his captives living and breathing, but very dead to who they were in God.

Read Daniel 1:6–19. Write the Jewish names of the four young men written about on the top line in the top cells. Then, write their Babylonian names on the top lines in the bottom cell.

These four golden exiles had Hebrew names that identified them with God. Daniel's name meant "God is my judge." Hananiah meant "God is gracious." Misha'el meant "Who is like God?" And Azariah meant "God has helped."

Write the meanings of these Hebrew names on the second line in the top cell.

One of the first things the king's eunuch did was change their names. Belteshazzar meant "protector of the King." Shadrach meant "commander of the Moon God." Meshach meant "What is what Aku is?" Abednego meant "Servant of Nabu."[23]

Write the meanings of these pagan names on the second line in the bottom cell.

What can you surmise is the point of changing their names?

My friend, we live in a proverbial Babylon. Oh, the names of the gods are different but be sure of this: the city that claimed our captives is a word picture and lesson for us.

Review your notes from this week's podcasts. Fill in the blanks below.

WE ARE ALL IN _____.

The Babylonian _____ is a picture of something
_____. We're all _____ to feel like we are
_____.

What similarities do you see between your modern world and the ancient land of Babylon? How do you see the human exile?

Be careful. The enemy has a plan for your time in Babylon, surely as God does. His is to steal, destroy, and ultimately to kill you (John 10:10). But he seems to always start with renaming you.

The enemy does not just want you to forget who God is. He seeks to create so much amnesia in your life that you aren't even sure who you are.

Some of the things Satan has tried to change my name to included "Whore," "Unusable," "Without Hope," "Hypocrite," and "Unwanted."

Let me tell you, it took nearly five decades for me to identify the last lie on my list. Probably because the enemy planted it when I was so young and tender.

At the age of four months, my baby brother became very ill. Aunts and uncles cared for me while my mom and dad cared for their infant son in the hospital. I distinctly remember standing in a parking lot with an aunt as we looked up to a hospital window where my mother and father were waving to me. My baby brother was in my mother's arms. What was meant to be a connection to my family, Satan used to cause disconnection. He whispered into my heart: "You don't belong."

By the time I was an adult, I always just kind of felt like I didn't belong. In friend groups. In my family. At Bible studies. On the stage. It even showed up in my marriage. There was always a sense that everyone would be content if I were just not in the picture. Or that I was not necessary. The lie never crippled me. I served Jesus well with my limp, but eventually I just wanted to be free!

In November of 2018, I was with a group of friends in the Dominican Republic. We had been sitting in God's presence and praying for many hours when my dear friend Lynn Nold asked me what I needed God to do in my heart and mind. I told her that I was feeling as if I didn't belong. (I write that as if it were easy. I assure you it was a battle to get those words out of my mouth.) I told my friends about my childhood memory.

Lynn asked God simply to help me see how my mother and father felt toward me when they were looking down at three-year-old Dannah in the parking lot. I was suddenly overwhelmed with love I have never known. My friends say I curled up like a child and began to cry like one, but they were tears of great joy. Of course, I'd been told many times by my mother how she felt. It's quite another thing for the Truth-filled voice of God to thunder it into your heart and mind. I was aware that the love I was feeling was from my mother and my father, but also from God.

I will never wear the name Unwanted again. For the rest of my living days, I will be like Daniel who did not take his Babylonian name. I know my identity. I am a Chosen Daughter (Eph. 1:3–8). I not only know this is my name. I *feel* it!

If you have forgotten who you are, I want to help you remember in your prayer time today.

For today's prayer activity, I want you to ask God to help you identify any names the enemy has given you and begin to replace them with God's Truth. Begin by sitting quietly and being mindful of any recurrent negative thoughts or emotions you struggle with that could be considered a name or label. Write them in the column on the left.

NAMES THE ENEMY TRIES TO GIVE ME	WHO GOD SAYS I AM

Next, take some time to pray. Ask God to reveal His Truth to you. If you need help, as I did, call a friend and ask them to pray with you. Your ultimate goal is to write the Truth in the column on the right and to include a verse of Scripture that you can treasure and meditate upon as you embrace your true identity.

Congratulations! You just studied and prayed for another week. Now, let's combine the two by meditating. Soak in what you've meditated on all week, allowing God's Spirit to direct your mind and heart to what He intends for you to embrace.

• *Ask God to identify a Bible verse or sentence that He is prompting you to embrace and understand. Write it in the space below.*

• *Reword that Bible verse or sentence into a prayer. Ask God what He wants you to do with it. Write a response to Him about what you sense Him saying. Determine in your heart to live it out.*

Is It OK to Question God?

Habakkuk used _____ to talk to God. In doing so, he lived up to ____ _____.

_____ _____
_____ _____
_____ _____

When it comes to questions, what determines if you are a wrestler or embracer? It's how you ask the question.

HEBREWS

TWO RESPONSES TO GOD'S PROPHECY

1. _____ the _____ and join the faithful in _____ on the _____ of _____.

2. _____ the _____ and _____ _____ the contagion of _____ _____.

Either way, you will have questions.

Habit #3: Remember to embed questions for God with truth.

Answers to the podcast fill-in-the-blanks can be found on page 215.

WEEK 3

Remember to Embed Questions with Truth

Corrie Ten Boom became the first licensed female watchmaker in Holland. She shared a business with her father, and they lived above their shop with her sister, Betsie.

When the Nazis invaded their country, the simplicity of life changed forever. Customers coming and going all day long made their watchmaker's shop the perfect location to hide Jews. So, they did. Up to six at a time. The trio helped nearly eight hundred people escape Germany's slaughter.

But it eventually cost the family.

They were carted off as captives to labor camps in 1944.

Corrie survived sleeping covered in fleas, laboring in harsh winter weather in thread bare clothing, and eating nothing more than porridge and a piece of bread each day. Her father and sister did not. But before Betsie died, she helped her sister wrestle with some questions.

Corrie had a lot of them.

And her dear ever-weakening sister always seemed to know how to find the answers. Corrie recalls:

> I remember one occasion when I was very discouraged there. Everything around us was dark, and there was darkness in my heart. I remember telling Betsie that I thought God had forgotten us.[1]

It seems so many who walk the path of faith have experienced times when they feel deserted. Abandoned by God Himself.

> "No, Corrie," said Betsie. "He has not forgotten us. Remember His Word: 'For as the heavens are high above the earth, so great is His steadfast love towards those who fear Him.'"
>
> Often, I have heard people say, 'How good God is! We prayed it would not rain for our church picnic and look at the lovely weather!' Yes, God is good when He sends good weather. But God was also good when He allowed my sister, Betsie, to starve to death before my eyes in a German concentration camp."[2]

Betsie taught Corrie to always check in with God's Word when the doubts and fears came. Corrie died free and happy at the age of ninety-one. On her birthday.

There is a Jewish fable that says celebrating the same day for both birth and death is a unique sign of someone very special.

I do not dabble in fables. In this one instance, however, it could be truth.

* * *

MEDITATION 1

How to bring your questions to God

Where were you on 9/11?

If you have to ask what I'm talking about, you're too young to remember the terror.

I was stranded at home without a car because mine was in the shop. But when the fourth plane crashed in rural Pennsylvania just one hundred miles from my backyard, I found someone to give me a ride to my kids' elementary school. (This mama bear wanted her children.)

I remember sitting in the teachers' lounge all afternoon.

I remember what I ate.

I remember who was there with me.

And I remember the first time I saw a picture of Osama bin Laden.

Terror has a way of cementing itself into our memory.

Americans lost 2,977 friends and family members that day. Six thousand were physically injured. Countless bear emotional scars to this day.

Imagine if the numbers were 30,000 dead and 50,000 injured.[3] What kind of emotional rubble does that leave behind?

Welcome to post–World War II London.

By 1953, medical doctor and minister Martin Lloyd Jones recognized the imprint war had left on his Westminster Chapel congregation. The city was rebuilding hearts and homes after suffering widespread damage as a result of aerial bombings.

And they just did not know how to talk to God in the middle of the rubble.

Jones pulled out an ancient book that contained the secrets of living by faith in evil times. It was written by a man who modeled how to talk to God when life hits hard. Turns out Habakkuk was just the tutor the congregation needed to get their prayers back on track.

If there's rubble of any kind in your life today, you could probably use a private lesson too.

I know a guy!

Let's dig in to learn from him today.

Look at Habakkuk 1:12–17. Read it and make observations.

Compare Habakkuk 1:2–3 to today's passage. Then, answer these questions.

What common type of sentence does Habakkuk employ in both of these passages?

What is different in the way he uses that form of communication?

What do you think has happened in the prophet's mind and heart between the two passages?

What began as wrestling softens slightly now as the embrace gentles and the prophet begins to cling to God.

Habakkuk the wrestler becomes Habakkuk the embracer.

—NANCY DEMOSS WOLGEMUTH[4]

Habakkuk is no longer just hurling questions at God, but now lacing them with respect. He's asking himself what he already knows to be true about God before he opens his mouth. And he's finding some solid ground to stand on.

When you have hard questions rolling through your mind, *that* is God speaking to you. He is not silent but is sending you a message, inviting you to know His character intimately in the current situation. Questions, when asked properly, can be a way of embracing God.

Many years ago, I had a lot of questions for God because of some devastating events in my personal life. My brain was mush. I couldn't read. Couldn't write. Didn't remember simple, important things—like to feed myself. (Thanks for reminding me, Mom!) I was exhausted, but hyper-vigilant so I could not sleep. Trying to comprehend the Bible and pray was futile. But I knew I needed those things.

I got a set of three-ring bound 3x5 cards. I wrote Romans 8:31–39 on the first card and determined that reading it aloud would be the extent of my daily time with God. That was as much as I could muster. (Little did I know I was practicing one of Habakkuk's most important habits.)

I began reading Romans 8:31–39 many times each day. Before I realized it, the sentences and phrases were showing up in my questions. *"Where are you, God"* evolved into a more robust: *"God, why does it feel like you are so distant if tribulation can't separate me from your love? Is that really true? Please show me."* I began to understand that no matter what happened, none of it would contain the power to separate me from the love of Christ. This Truth became real to me in a way I had not known previously.

HARD QUESTIONS ARE INVITATIONS TO STAND ON THE FOUNDATION OF WHAT YOU ALREADY KNOW ABOUT GOD.

When you temper your doubts and questions with the Truth you already know, you begin to experience that character of God profoundly. Let's look at how Habakkuk practiced this.

Look at Habakkuk 1:12. Underline the question the prophet asks God. Double underline the words of respect the prophet uses in the verse.

*How might these be evidence that the way Habakkuk presents the question is **rhetorical** and inquisitive, and that he is choosing to stand on what he does know to be true about God?*

The Six Habits of Living by Faith

Turn to the back of your book. You'll find the six practices or habits of living by faith that Habakkuk demonstrated. Review that list again.

Here are habits one through three. Circle key words that will help you remember the action you need to take for each of them.

1. Remember to wrestle with God when He seems silent.

2. Remember to look to see where God is at work.

3. Remember to embed questions for God with Truth.

Write the key words or phrases of the first three habits on the following lines.

_____

_____

_____

THE PROPER WAY TO ASK A QUESTION

The proper way to question God is as easy as 1, 2, 3. Here's how it works.

1. **Ask God your hard questions *respectfully*.** Present them with an attitude that's inquisitive and willing to learn from God, even if full of sadness and confusion.

Look up these verses and jot down any insight they give you about questioning God.

James 1:5–6

Hebrews 4:16

Isaiah 55:8–9

God does not have any obligation to make sense to you. He is God. You are not. It should not be surprising when you don't understand your circumstances or see how God is working in something. But with a proper attitude, you can speak any question out to God when it comes to mind.

2. **Identify a Truth of God that you can believe.** Ask yourself: what is one thing that I know to be true? Just one. During times of testing, we often need to return to the basics and remember Truths that we have not needed in some time.

Look up these verses and make notes about the power of God's Word.

Numbers 23:19

2 Corinthians 1:20

John 8:31–32

Satan wants to make your questions a tool of your captivity. He can do that if you dwell on them, as they can begin to grow into doubt and faithless fearfulness. God's desire is that they'd lead you to freedom. To experience that, you must confront the question with His Truth. Let the years of becoming familiar with the Scriptures flood your mind, inviting God's Spirit to direct you to the one(s) you need for this testing. (If you are a new believer, ask a mentor to help you.) When nothing seems certain, remind yourself of at least one thing that is unchanging.

3. **Stand on the Truth.** When you find a Truth to stand on, it will likely be either a promise or a command. Apply what you know to be true to your problem. This may mean just frequently reminding yourself of a promise, or it could require you to obey a command of God. If there is a practical way to act on it, do it. This is how you plant your foot on the solid foundation of His Truth and stand firm.

Look up these verses and record any encouragement or directives as it relates to acting on God's Word.

James 1:22

John 14:21

Hebrews 4:12

I cannot emphasize enough what a difference this makes in your emotional state even if your circumstances do not shift. But the best way to know that is to experience it. So, give it a try during our prayer activity.

For today's prayer activity, I'd like you to take one or two of your *why* questions to God using the process I just taught you.

What are some of your why *questions? Write a few of them below on the left.*

MY QUESTIONS	GOD'S TRUTH

Now, search your mental Rolodex of God's Truth. (If you do not have many verses memorized, you can use some online search tools to find "promises of God" or "commands of God.") Even if you cannot see how they relate, write them above on the right.

How can you stand on one or more of these Truths this week?

Write a prayer to God expressing your desire to handle the questions of your heart well and your intention to stand on this Truth.

Embedding your questions with truth

Imagine you've been bleeding for twelve years. People smell your heavy menstrual rags before they see you.

And walk the other way.

You are considered untouchable. Unclean. And everyone is tired of your need. There's nothing that can be done.

But you hear about an unconventional new treatment. It would require you to travel a little and do something that's considered socially unacceptable, but that ridicule could not possibly be as bad as this.

Anything would be better than this.

So, you wait until the man from Nazareth is close. For others to touch you is forbidden, but to touch someone else? Unthinkable. Insane! But you believe what you've heard. This man reaches for the untouchables. And makes them clean.

The crowd is pressed in against Jesus. You lean low to the ground past the feet of the others and … just barely touch the hem of His robe.

You can feel it right away.

The ache abruptly ends. It feels like even the swelling is gone. And—you sniff the air—you can smell the dust of the ground and the sweat of the crowd, but not your own stench.

You are healed.

You don't know it yet, but people will follow your example. They'll do what you've just done. They'll sneak up on the crowd and grasp Christ's garment.

And they will be made clean too.

> . . . and [those that recognized Jesus] implored him that they might only touch the fringe of his garment. And as many as touched it were made well.
> (MATT. 14:36)

My friend, come close today. Touch the hem of our Savior's garment and see what healing He has for you.

For today's study activity, we will take one more look at Habakkuk 1:12–17. We'll need a fine-tooth comb to thoroughly search the strands of truth. Begin by drawing a crown above any qualities or truths about God that Habakkuk references. We're looking for a total of five, though I needed help to find two of them, I'll help you.

The questions in this portion of Habakkuk's conversation with God mingle his questions with specific truths he knows about God. This positions him to stand on them, almost as if he is reminding God about them in the hope that He might use those qualities to solve the problems of Judah.

This list of five qualities is from Martin Lloyd Jones's book *From Fear to Faith: Rejoicing in the Lord in Turbulent Times*[5] in which he dissected Habakkuk's book for his congregation in post-World War II London. Let's look at each of these characteristics of God more closely and determine how these truths might also be treasures you can lean into.

GOD IS ETERNAL (V. 12)

God exists outside the confines of time. Moses wrote that "a thousand years in your sight are like a day . . ." (Ps. 90:4a NIV). The apostle Peter actually cautioned his readers not to forget to remember how God sees time (2 Peter 3:8).

How might this be significant as you face your own devastating circumstances?

It may seem that it is taking a long time for God to answer your questions and solve your problems, but the way He sees time is different. His solution *is*. It just exists. Because He has already done the work and is doing it even now.

As we examine each of these attributes of God, I want you to think back on all the diligent studying you've been doing and consider why each quality is important to Habakkuk and the nation of Judah as they approach exile.

Let's tackle the first one: why do you think Habakkuk chose to mention God's eternal quality?

GOD IS SELF-EXISTENT (V. 12)

Anytime you see the word LORD in all capitals within Scripture, it is a translation of YHWH—an abbreviation of His Hebrew name Yahweh, sometimes translated as Jehovah.

How might using this name signify yet again that Habakkuk is softening in his wrestler's grip?

The name essentially means "The Self Existent."[6] God is. He was. He always will be. It is this name and quality that God uses to reveal Himself to Moses at the burning bush when He says, "I AM WHO I AM" (Ex. 3:14). When the Jewish people were in captivity to Egypt and crying out to Him for deliverance, God showed up to announce His self-existence. In other words, He is not dependent on anything or anyone in the world. When He is at work, He often invites us to be a part of it out of love. But never imagine for one second that the God of the universe *needs* you to fulfill His plans. If you go the way of Jonah and never turn back, He will accomplish whatever He desires.

How is this truth about God helpful for you as you wait on Him for answers and solutions to your own problems?

Why do you think Habakkuk chose to mention God's self-existence?

GOD IS HOLY (V. 13)

Generally, we equate holiness with moral goodness. But the quality as it relates to God is much bigger and speaks to His powerful ability to make right everything that is wrong. Kind of like the sun in our solar system is a force of light that penetrates all darkness.[7]

An attribute of God's holiness is referenced in verse 13. What words does it use, and how would you define the key word and its interaction with God's holiness?

Purity was no small thing for the Israelites who had rituals to avoid anything unclean or related to death. They could not touch a dead animal, for example. They had lists and lists of things that they could and could not do in order to stay morally clean. If anyone tried to enter the sacred Holy of Holies in God's Temple without being both permitted and ritualistically pure, they would die. (They actually tied a rope around the priests when they went in there. Morbid, huh?) Key action: do *not* touch.

But the prophet Isaiah turns all that thinking upside down when he receives a revelation from God. Like Habakkuk, his writing recognizes Jewish exile but has a longer lens to foretell the coming of Jesus Christ, who will change everything. Including how we become holy. To help Isaiah understand, God gives him a vision of coming into His throne room. Isaiah declares, "Woe is me. I am unclean." (He's pretty sure he's as good as dead.) Then, something new happens. God holds a coal and touches it to the prophet's lips. Instead of dying, He becomes clean (Isa. 6). This is symbolic of what Jesus will do when He touches individuals with leprosy, the woman with the issue of blood, a very-recently dead Lazarus, and others He heals during His time on earth. All unclean by Jewish ritual. But Jesus touches them. And it makes them clean. (That's what His life and death would do for us, too.) Key action: *do* touch!

When it comes to evil in this world, holiness matters. Why? Because everything—every circumstance, place, and person—is made right by His presence. This means your addiction, pain, failures, and sadness do not get to have the last say. A genocide, holocaust, exile, or nuclear bomb does not get to infuse the rest of the world with evil. The amazing work God does when He touches them will re-frame the way we see and experience everything. Unbelievably, He will make them useful and good for us (Rom. 8:28).

How does that make you feel about your problems? The evil and suffering you see in this world?

Why do you think Habakkuk mentions God's holiness as he presents his questions?

GOD IS MIGHTY (VV. 12–17)

Some versions make this quality of God's character easier to see. The word *mighty* is sometimes used to define the word *rock* in this passage. The visual picture of God as a rock, or rock of salvation, abounds in Scripture.

How is a rock mighty?

In Old Testament times, people would often hide in caves or mountain crevices from their enemies (1 Sam. 13:6; 22:1–5). When God says that He is their rock, it is a promise that He is a safe place to hide and to rest (Deut. 32:15; 2 Sam. 22:47; Ps. 89:26; 95:1).

The picture gets more beautiful as the prophets of the Old Testament begin to refer to their coming Messiah as a stone. Habakkuk would have heard Isaiah's prophecy: "But to Israel and Judah he will be a stone . . . a rock . . ." He warned that He would be a stone that was rejected by the builders but would become a cornerstone or anchor for the building anyway (Isa. 28:16). This idea of Jesus being a rock and a stone carries on throughout the New Testament.

Think specifically of a difficult relationship or painful problem you have faced. How was Jesus your rock?

What is Habakkuk possibly thinking when he uses this terminology to petition God on behalf of Judah?

GOD IS FAITHFUL (V. 12)

Draw a rainbow above the word my *as it appears in verse 12. What does this mean? Why is Habakkuk personalizing the attributes of God? (The rainbow should be a big clue.)*

Matthew Poole's Commentary claims that when Habakkuk uses possessive plural pronouns, "He refers to the ancient covenant relation which God had taken them into, and implies his hope and expectation of help from God . . ."[8] The possessive language of the prophets is often their subtle reminder—either to God or themselves—of the great power and hope of covenant. Habakkuk is saying, "We are yours."

Another hint at covenant language is the title LORD or YHWH, which is used as God's covenant name throughout the Old Testament. We'll look more at the power of covenant tomorrow. Let's stay focused on faithfulness today, but know that this attribute is rooted in, expressed in, and guaranteed by the ancient unbreakable covenant God made with the Jewish nation long ago.

Look up the verses below and surmise why God's faithfulness is such good news for Judah. And for us.

Romans 3:3

2 Timothy 2:13

Those two truths from the New Testament have been stood on a time or two by this sinful woman. I pray them often. "Oh, God, thank You that nothing I do can nullify Your faithfulness. Thank You that Your faithfulness is not just something You do, but who You are. And You cannot disown Yourself."

Why did Habakkuk mention God's faithfulness?

In the face of difficult times, the questions of our heart require us to look back at God's faithfulness and rest in it until we once again see it rising to our need. We can either fixate on our current trial and become anxious, or meditate on past provision and experience peace. Perhaps that is one reason we face challenges, so we will pause to remember what God has already done for us.

I invite you to do that right now.

Consider God's faithfulness. A good way to do this is to write a list remembering how He's shown up for you in the past. I did this the day I realized the high-risk nature of my son and daughter-in-law's first pregnancy. I wrote for pages and pages. Here's a snippet.

February 27–2 little girls! Yesterday Robby and Aleigha told us they're having twins. …But Jesus, we need you to vigilantly watch over them. I remember . . .

. . . You healed my baby brother.

. . . You saved my father's life in Russia.

. . . You gave my mother a bye from cancer.

. . . You restored my broken heart.

. . . You found us a daughter who needed a home and rescued Autumn.

. . . You rescued our marriage.

. . . You even healed Cindy Lou Who [my sweet mini-fainting goat.]

DO IT AGAIN, LORD!

Write a similar prayer remembering all the ways that He has touched your life in the past. Remember His faithfulness. And ask Him to do it again.

MEDITATION 3

The truth you need while you wait for answers

FAST FORWARD TO BABYLON >>>

Imagine for just a moment that you are in a relationship with the love of your life. How he makes your heart happy. Until he doesn't. You knew he was growing distant but did not realize just how far he would go. The betrayal leaves you unable to sleep at night and yet wishing you could sleep the day out every morning. You eat grief for breakfast, lunch, and dinner but have no appetite for much else.

How could he do this?

You are that lover.

So am I.

We make God's heart so happy, and then we slowly grow distant. Again and again. How ironic is it that we question God—His faithfulness, His presence, His deliverance—when we are so prone to wander?

Let's bravely examine our own *un*faithfulness today.

Read Habakkuk 1:12–17 again. Add any new observations that come to mind.

Is it just me, or does Habakkuk have an awful lot to say about sea creatures and nets in Habakkuk 1:12–17? (Something smells *fishy* to me, but I think we can *scale* this mystery and pull up some understanding from *overboard*.)

When you see any recurring thread in a passage of Scripture, it's wise to dig a little bit to see why it's there.

Draw a little Christian fish symbol above any nouns in the passage that seem to refer to fish or fishing. Then, answer these questions.

How many did you find?

Who do you think these fish represent?

What do you think is being described?

If a fish is taken out of water, placed in nets, and dragged somewhere on the earth, what will the result be?

Summarize—in good old-fashioned narrative with subjects, verbs, and direct objects—what Habakkuk is saying in his symbolic poem.

Victorious kings of the ancient world would march captives off in long lines. They were strung together with hooks in their lips tethering them to one another. Just like fish. Evidence of this has been found in many archeological discoveries found in the ruins of ancient Assyria.[9] Is it possible Daniel and the other captives were carted off in this manner which was as common as handcuffs are today?

What God showed Habakkuk in a vision or revelation was graphic, humiliating, and hopeless. No wonder he had so many questions. Let's not whitewash the book of Daniel, which as we learned last week gives us a glimpse into the days of the Babylonian captivity when our prophet's words proved to be true.

In addition to being strung up like fish, Daniel and his friends must have been exhausted by the time we find them on the pages of Scripture. It's unlikely that a tour bus picked them up for the roughly 900-mile trip[10] from Jerusalem to Babylon. You can imagine they planted one weary foot in front of the other for months to make the journey. Make no mistake, they were fully aware that they were captives in bondage.

And they probably had a lot of questions.

How could God let Babylon overthrow His people in such a horrific way?

What happened to my mom and dad? Brothers and sisters?

Will I ever stop seeing these violent pictures of the attack in my head?

How long until we get to go home?

Why, God?

STANDING ON TRUTH IN BABYLON

Let's pop back into Babylon for the rest of today. Daniel, Shadrach, Meshach, and Abednego— who are likely teenage boys—have been sequestered in the king's palace for indoctrination.

Compare these two Bible verses:

DANIEL 9:2	JEREMIAH 25:12

What can we conclude? Daniel had Truth memorized and at-the-ready! Let's see how this young man uses it.

Review the three-step plan for how to pray when you're devastated.

Fill in the blanks based on what you studied yesterday.

1. Ask God your hard _____ _____.

2. Identify one _____ _____ _____ you can believe in.

3. Stand on that _____.

Now read Daniel 1: 8–16 and answer these questions.

What is the familiar problem that Daniel and his friends faced right off the bat in Babylon?

Why did they not want to do it? What questions might they have struggled with?

What truth from the Torah (first five books of the Bible) might Daniel and his friends have floating around in their memories to navigate this first problem? (Use your logic and an online concordance.)

What verb does the first verse in this passage use to describe how Daniel responded?

Daniel and the guys could smell that roasted pig. In their culture, anytime there was meat on the table, there had been worship in a temple. (Gives a whole new meaning to "pigging out!") The wine was understood to be a proper inclusion for idol worship. This wasn't just dinner, but a pagan feast in honor of Babylonian gods.

Daniel calls for a huddle. He asks the guys to search their mental Rolodexes for what they needed—Truth. I imagine he might read his out loud as he rolls them through his mind.

Hmm …. Let's see: here's one thing we know. We don't eat pork (Lev. 11:7, 8). Oh, this one might come in handy. Remember, that wine has been a gateway drug to the intoxicating addiction of idol worship for our grandparents (Ex. 34:15; Num. 25:5). And what else? Um. Ah. Wait! I found the one I need: Yahweh promised He Himself would be with us wherever we went and that we don't need to be afraid (Deut. 31:8).

His devastating circumstances and the questions they produced led Daniel to Truth that was rock solid. And standing on it told him how to act. Eventually, the resolve and discipline paid off.

Read Daniel 1:17–20. What does it say was the result of the famous fast?

I do not think Daniel all of a sudden resolved to do the right thing. This was no New Year's resolution intended to get him back on track. He'd been training for a moment like this his whole life.

Becoming exceptional is never an all-of-a-sudden event.

Malcolm Gladwell analyzed what makes people exceptional in his book *Outliers*. From the Beatles to Bill Gates, he tried to find the common denominator of greatness. His hotly debated discovery is The 10,000 Hour Rule, which states that people who excel have disciplined themselves into their expertise by diligently spending about twenty hours a week learning their trade.[11] These are people who did not mindlessly go along with the crowd's choices and behavior.

I've compiled a list of some of the activities into which Americans invest close to or more than twenty hours a week. Circle any that seem accurate of you.

Scrolling through social media (21 hours)[12]

Shopping online (20 hours)[13]

Watching Netflix, Hulu, and Amazon (20 hours)[14]

Eating, food prep,[15] and thinking about eating[16] (15 hours)

Does the time you spend doing those things increase when you're in a painful or difficult season of questions?

Look at what you've circled. Is that what you want to be known for? Is that where you want to excel? Or is God calling you to something higher?

MAKE A RESOLUTION

Maybe, like Daniel, you are simply a resolute individual. I am not.

For example, spending and feasting in December is something I have not been able to experience without my flesh taking over. Before I know it, I might not only decorate for Christmas but nigh unto re-decorate my entire house! (That actually happened once.) Somehow, the holiday always seems to squeeze the "Christ-in-me" right out of me. Can you identify?

So, every January I do something to push reset on my appetites. I participate in a 21-day Daniel fast, primarily for the purpose of remembering I am capable of self-control. I give my spirit an opportunity to tell my flesh who's boss.

When I fast, I petition God for something specific, and this year is the first time I'm asking Him to do something that is not all about me. (Can you say breakthrough?) I generally ask Him to move in *my* family, *my* ministry, *my* health, or *my* relationships. But sometime in November of 2019, God prompted my heart to call an army of mothers and grandmothers to fast to break the bondage of anxiety and depression in our nation. I'm kicking this year off with a burden for at least one nation. Mine. This shift in my heart has been—in part—due to the many hours I have spent studying Habakkuk.

What are you going to spend twenty hours practicing this week?

You aren't going to get to phone this one in. Check out your prayer homework for today.

For today's prayer activity, I encourage you to make a resolution to change the way you feast on this world. Whatever appetite God has revealed to be out of control, consider muscling up with some self-discipline. This could mean shutting down The 'Gram, not spending money on anything but essentials, or entering into a food fast.

Daniel told the king's eunuch to give him ten days before making a judgment concerning the impact of self-control. So, I challenge you to do whatever God calls you to do for the next ten days.

Use your prayer time today to let God search your heart and write a commitment to Him about how you will enter into self-discipline for the sake of putting your spirit, and ultimately His, in control of your daily actions.

MEDITATION 4

Answering questions about the truth

One decade ago, my very dear friend Nancy DeMoss Wolgemuth was delivering a message on Habakkuk. She paraphrased the passage we will study today into a prayer for our times.

> Lord, human effort isn't cutting it. Oh, it can give us mega-churches. It can give us multi-million-dollar ministries. It can get us on radio and TV and publish books. Lord, we want to see **Your** power. We want to see what only **You** can do. We don't want to settle for what man can do. Lord, revive **Your** work.[17]

For many decades, American Christians have adopted the same customs, behaviors, and patterns of the culture in the name of ministry. While I think some of that is useful, is it possible that we've gone too far and have been doing things in our own power?

In recent years, mega-churches were emptying. The mass exodus was so significant that *The Atlantic* published an article titled "America's Epidemic of Empty Churches."[18]

Some authors who were riding the wave of Christian celebrity status when Nancy originally prayed those words have either recanted their faith or have taken a razor blade to their Bibles to cut out what they don't like.

Many multi-million-dollar ministries have crumbled, having leaders whose moral and financial ethics were found wanting. The wreckage was headline fodder for the likes of *The New York Times*.

And then.

A new virus emerged resulting in a global pandemic.

With the gods of culture quieted by empty public spaces and spiritual fervor awakened by desperate need, the churched began to meet online and in small home groups with burgeoning attendance. Even the secular media noticed. *The Wall Street Journal* published an article with a headline that posed a question: "A Coronavirus Great Awakening? Sometimes the most important ingredient for spiritual renewal is a cataclysmic event."[19]

In the midst of global ground zero, the world paused to remember God.

Read Habakkuk 3:2 and jot down your observations. (No, you didn't miss an entire chapter of the book of Habakkuk. And yes, I skipped chapter two. We will pick up our studies there next week.)

Rewrite this piece of poetry into a simple, direct sentence from Habakkuk to God.

Do you think this is a request even though it is not in the form of a question?

What does Habakkuk want revived? When?

In chapter 1, Habakkuk's questions are focused on Judah. How has his focus shifted in this verse?

My first thought when I read this passage was this: "How fitting a prayer this is for our modern world!"

Habakkuk cried out to God to work "in the midst of the years." He's asking the Lord to show Himself, as one commentator puts it, *during* the "calamity in which we live. Now that our calamities are at their height."[20] Even though the disaster of his day revealed God's anger, Habakkuk begged for mercy and the might of God's works to be revealed during the foretold judgment.

He's no longer crying out for God to do just anything. At the realization that his world is changing dramatically, the prophet comes to crave revival.

When you think about it, the request is audacious! Not only does Habakkuk want God to show up at the peak of the problem, but he wants Him to favor them with revival. How is it that he could be so bold? I'm glad you asked.

verb. To return to consciousness or life; become active or flourishing again.

transitive verb. To restore from a depressed, inactive, or unused state; bring back.[21]

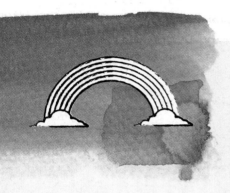

COVENANT FOR DUMMIES

Draw rainbows above any words in Habakkuk 3:2 that might be a reference to *covenant*. (Look back at page 94 to see what we discovered about the topic when learning about God's faithfulness.) You may not get them all. As we study today, go back and add rainbows to any words you miss.

Take a stab at coming up with a definition of the word covenant.

It is difficult for us to define a word when we have almost no context for it in our society. Our closest related word is *contract,* but that pales in comparison to the richness of a complex partnership that the ancient Hebrew world understood *covenant* to represent. It was a legally binding agreement, but not just a transaction. It was also a relationship.

> ## *A covenant is a relationship that is a stunning blend of law and love.*
> —TIM KELLER[22]

Commentator David Baker writes this about the verses we're focusing on today:

Habakkuk calls on God to remember and exhibit the merciful side of his character . . . . This term is used elsewhere of God's covenant grace to people who acknowledge him (Genesis 8:1, 9:15; Nehemiah 1:8; Job 14:13; Luke 1:54, 72). The love of God is so strong that even when he is flagrantly ignored, deserted or rejected, he is drawn, as a husband to his wife, or a mother to her child, to love in spite of the actions of the other (Isaiah 1:2, 18–20; Hosea 11:8–11). The wrongs are real, but so too are the compassion and desire to forgive, if the "condition" for restoration—a renewed desire to acknowledge God—is present to allow the floods of his mercy to be unleashed.[23]

Underline the following words in the paragraph above: "a renewed desire to acknowledge God." How have you witnessed that in your corner of the world lately?

Habakkuk's no longer thinking about himself and his people, but God's work. God's fame. God's headlines.

There is not just one covenant. There are several referenced in the Old Testament, and tomorrow we'll study the New Testament covenant. The holy agreements sort of build on and perfect one another. Collectively they are an overriding relationship drenched in the faithfulness of God. But I find the account of Abram's commencement to be most educational.

Read Genesis 15:1–21 and answer the following questions.

What is troubling Abram as he talks with God? And what promise does God make to him?

(Ironic bonus question: from what land did God bring Abram? _____)

What does God ask Abram to do to establish a covenant relationship? What does God do?

How does Abram respond when birds of prey come down on the dead animals he is preparing for the covenant ceremony?

What happened to Abram when the sun went down?

Describe the elements that passed through the pieces of animal flesh.

Now, unless you've spent some time studying *covenant*, it's difficult to understand what's really happening. But let's try.

R.C. Sproul provides us with historical context for the way such partnerships were made in Old Testament times:

> When covenants were made in the ancient Near East, certain rites would accompany the agreement in order to signify what would happen if one or both parties failed to live up to their end of the pact. One common ritual involved dismembering animals and then laying the pieces in two rows side-by-side with a path in between. The individuals making the covenant would then pass between the animals and invoke a curse upon themselves if they broke the agreement. In performing this rite both parties were in effect saying, "If I do not fulfill the terms of this covenant, may the destruction that befell these animals also be upon my head."[24]

Through the pages of the Bible, we are witness to a remarkable occurrence in Abram's covenant ceremony. **Only God walked through this sacrifice of animals. Abram did not.** Abram was asleep when God—appearing in the form of a "smoking fire pot" and "flaming torch"[25]—passed through the broken animal pieces. Essentially, He was saying, "If this covenant is broken—and it will be—may I be as these bloodied sacrificed animals."

To someone living in the covenant age, this would have been unthinkable.

Maybe, but *just* maybe, the lesser partner in a covenant would pass alone through the pieces as they were the one that needed the leg up. But never would the greater party walk alone through them. It would not make sense to anyone who understood covenant to think of the more powerful and provisional party not being able to fulfill their covenant obligations.

Faithful?

We have no comprehension just how faithful our God is to us. He anticipated His people's inability to be faithful and walked through those bloody pieces anyway.

COVENANT KEEPERS

Habakkuk had a complete understanding of God's covenant faithfulness. And he called upon it in times of great difficulty. So should we. This enables the answers to our questions to be deeply rooted in Truth.

You see, there are facts and there is Truth. Fact: Judah was going to be taken captive by Babylon. Truth: Judah's covenant God would be faithful though they had not been.

You try it. Write one fact you are facing right now and then a Truth you can hold on to.

Fact:

Truth:

When Nebuchadnezzar came to carry God's chosen people away as prophesied, Judah's most faithful were trained and ready to walk in the hope of unfailing love. Fully aware of God's covenant promises, they rested in His faithfulness every step of the way to Babylon. And every day within its walls.

How did they know to hold on to this hope? It'd been passed on like an Olympic torch. From the baton of one faithful heart to another, the unfailing love and mercy of God was heralded.

And now, that holy flame of Truth is in our hands. What will we do with it?

In an effort to take our eyes off our own personal needs and to intercede for the glory of God to be revealed in our world, I'd like to encourage you to intercede for the nation of Israel (Judah) today. Below are some verses from the Bible that can guide us in praying for God's chosen people. Use these to write a prayer.

- Pray for the peace of Jerusalem. (Ps. 122:6)
- Thank God for His everlasting covenant with Israel. (Gen. 17:7, 9)
- God gave His people the land of Israel as an eternal possession.

Pray for that fulfillment to the end of time. (Gen. 15; 17:7–8; 48:4; Ps. 105:7–11)

• Thank God that His judgments do not void His covenant and that a people's lack of faith does not nullify His faithfulness. (Ezek. 37; Rom. 3:3)

• Pray for the Jewish people to accept Jesus as their Messiah. (Rom. 1:16)

MEDITATION 5

The ultimate answer

FAST FORWARD TO BABYLON

Jesus promised that as long as we have feet on this sin-encrusted sod, we would "have trouble" (John 16:33 NIV). The wrestling and embracing you are doing during painful times in your life right now are practice for the next difficult trial you face.

But there's a bigger picture that we must keep in view. Like Habakkuk, we have received "notice." God, in His Word, guarantees that Christ will indeed return. Just as Habakkuk had knowledge of events that awaited an appointed time, so do we. It's possible you and I will be here on this earth for some dark and harrowing "last days" when humankind's vices of conceit, brutality, and unholiness (and the list goes on) will intensify (2 Tim. 3:1–5). God's people must be mentally, emotionally, and spiritually prepared for these "terrible times" (v. 1 NIV).

We also may *not* be here for that cataclysmic event. No one knows when it will happen but God Himself (Matt. 24:36). Regardless, we must be faithful to pass on to future generations the training to live righteously by faith through evil times so they are prepared to face "great distress, unequaled from the beginning of the world until now—and never to be equaled again" (Matt. 24:21 NIV).

If ever there will be questions on the hearts and minds of believers, it will be then. If we do not pass on the baton of Truth, they'll likely believe the facts will have the final say. I assure you, they will not.

My dear friend Donna VanLiere has a burden to wake us up from our complacency toward this responsibility. She's used her incredible gift of writing fiction to help us gain understanding about the challenging days preceding Christ's return in a book titled *The Time of Jacob's Trouble*. The true gift is that the second half of her work contains a biblical explanation of the narrative, where she writes:

> . . . one-fourth of the Bible is being overlooked. Who would pick up the latest bestseller and not read twenty-seven percent of the book? If you were reading a book, would you read a few pages and then skip to somewhere in the middle, and then skip some more pages, not even bothering to read the end? I doubt you would, but that's the way many people read Scripture. How can they tie all of God's Word together without reading that twenty-seven percent?[26]

We cannot study Habakkuk's poetry without a growing awareness that it's just one piece of the unfolding story of God's love for humanity.

For today's study activity, we'll pause our direct study of Habakkuk. With a fresh understanding of covenant in our minds, let's dig into the New Covenant of Jesus Christ which is the one offered to you and me. Write down any observations you have when you read Hebrews 9:11–28, with a focus on verse 15.

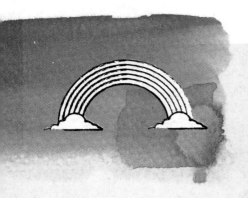

What is Christ called in Hebrews 9:15?

A mediator facilitates communication between two parties who are in conflict. Humanity has been in conflict with God due to our sinful nature. Christ mediates between us with a new covenant.

What does Christ use as His mediation tool?

Why does it require a covenant sacrifice? (See verses 12–14, 22.)

What two physical appearances of Christ do verses 26 and 28 foretell? List them below:

1 •

2 •

HABAKKUK AND HIS FELLOW PROPHETS HAD GREAT VISION

Habakkuk and his contemporaries saw Jerusalem's fall and their own people's coming captivity in visions they received from God. They could also see God's deliverance, as He would come up against Babylon and other nations that harmed His beloved. They held onto the covenant faithfulness of God as they awaited the deliverance.

These prophets did not suffer from near-sightedness. Many of them, including our friend Daniel, had revelations concerning events that have yet to happen on the timeline of eternity. They saw beyond the mini-deliverances to an ultimate one. It is this kind of vision I would like to help you embrace today.

● ● ●

TIME FOR TIMELINES!
Turn to pages 222–223 in the back of the book.

Find "The Time of the Church" and make a "You Are Here" red dot.

You know those big red dots you find on the directory of a mall or amusement park? The ones that say, "You are here!" Draw one right above that cute church. It's where you and I show up in this cosmic story.

On either side of us are the two appearances, or comings, of Christ wherein He first mediates our covenant and then seals it.

1st • Christ our Savior. The Son of God was born as a human baby to remain sinless that He might mediate a covenant on our behalf with His life. All of the prophecies about the first appearance of Christ as our Savior have come true, and that's no mathematical probability. It's been estimated that the chances of that much accuracy is 1 in 100,000,000,000,000,000. That's 10 to the 17th power. (I'm fairly allergic to math, but I'm able to understand that the probability of these prophecies coming true was . . . well, improbable.)

Unless it was God's sovereignty at work.

Find the cross and write "Christ our Savior" above it.

2nd • Christ our Coming King. Jesus died, rose from the grave, and ascended into heaven to be seated with God the Father. One day He will return to seal our covenant and redeem all of creation.

Find the lamb with a flag and write "Christ our Coming King" above it.

Here's where we get to adjust our vision so that we can have faith like Habakkuk as he was living in difficult times and became aware that there was more evil to come.

Hearing the prophecy of Judah's exile? Dress rehearsal.

The real test of faith would begin when what Habakkuk and others foretold unfolded during the Babylonian exile of Judah. The writings of many prophets would provide the strength training for young men like Daniel, Shadrach, Meshach, and Abednego to live by faith in evil days.

The lessons we can learn from them are practical and invaluable. With our eyes fixed on the future, let's head backwards to ancient Babylon. We'll use the book of Daniel to adjust our spiritual eyes because he was entrusted by God with a prophecy that could come true in *our lifetime.*

Upon arrival in Babylon, you'll find things have changed a great deal. King Nebuchadnezzar has died peacefully in his sleep. Persia has taken over Babylon. And Daniel? He's no strapping fifteen-year-old with impressive physical qualities, but a weakening eighty-year-old. He still lives in Babylon despite the fact that King Cyrus has allowed the Jews to return to Jerusalem.

In the passage we'll look at today, either a theophany (Christ Himself) or an angel—scholars are divided—brings Daniel a vision. We're not going to get down into the weeds of these words, but we'll do a fly-by to see the overall terrain. Turn to Daniel chapter 10.

Read verse 14. What do we know about what Daniel saw?

Read verses 1–3, 7–8, 16–17. What is the prophet's response to what he sees?

Read Daniel 12:4. Record what Daniel is instructed to do with what he sees.

Do you respond like Daniel when you read about what will happen to people you may not even know in the future? Do you respond that way when you read about what is happening to people in other countries right now? I don't know about you, but I could use a good infusion of Daniel's empathy by way of a holy transfusion. Let's try to get one today.

OUR COMING SAVIOR

Read Revelation 5:1–10 where John has recorded a revelation for you and me concerning the end times. What is the angel asking?

Write down specific qualities and names used to describe the One who is able to do what the angel asks.

What tribe is given honor in one of these names? How will that honor the faithfulness of Habakkuk, Daniel, and others who believed in things although they could not see them?

Jesus is both a Lion and a Lamb. But when He wins this final battle for you and for me, He'll do it as the Lamb.

Draw a picture of what the Lamb looks like. Based on what little we know in verse six, take time to really meditate on how it looks.

When Jesus enters into the final battle, He will still bear the scars of the blood covenant mediation.

Our Lamb.

Who died.

He can open the scroll.

It was His sinless life that enabled Him to be a spotless *covenant* sacrifice for you and me on Calvary. **This qualifies Him to open the scroll and break the seals.**

WHY DOES THAT MATTER?

We will attempt to explore that a bit more as we continue our study of Habakkuk next week, but let me be honest. We don't really know why this opening of the scroll matters, but it does. Very much.

John is greatly burdened (v. 4) when no one can open the scroll. He sees and feels things we do not. He weeps and weeps. What could he understand that we do not?

One possibility is that the scroll is a sort of deed to the property ("nations") of the world. Ancient deeds often had writing on the outside and were sealed. The only ones who could open them to read the insides were the rightful owners.[27]

Another idea is that it was the Lamb's book of life which contained the names of those who would be granted eternal life and that the names were so numerous they did not all fit inside.[28] Daniel wrote about a book that could not be opened too. We just read those verses in chapter 12 of the book he wrote while in Babylonian exile. Could John be seeing the same book in his revelation and why it is so upsetting? Was Daniel grieved at how many names were missing? Or that people could not be released into heaven if no one could open that scroll?

Whatever it is, there is One who can open it. Only Jesus is worthy to open it to see what's inside. When Jesus comes forward and removes the seven seals, there is a celebration of sorts and a loud voice says that the kingdoms of the world have become the kingdoms of our LORD (Yahweh) and His Christ!

It's possible that this is the moment of all moments that matters the most. The one where Satan finally surrenders his counterclaim on the world. And on me. And you.

Whatever it is, it matters.

For today's prayer activity, I want you to consider something, but before you read ahead, please pause to let God speak to you about Revelation 5:1–10. One way to do this is to use a song that reflects it back to you.

PAUSE TO REFLECT

Listen to "Is He Worthy?" by Andrew Peterson.[29]

Now, write your prayer to God. Talk to Him about your thoughts and feelings concerning events and prophecies that may not involve you or those you love. Consider: Are you more like Daniel, Habakkuk, and John who weep for those who will experience them? Or are you like Hezekiah (whom I taught on during this week's podcast) when you consider events that are to happen in the future? Why do you think you respond that way, and do you want to change in any way? Write to God about your heart concerning these matters.

Congratulations! You have completed another week of rather complex thinking and studying. Take some time to allow God's Spirit to direct your mind and heart to what He intends for you to embrace from your time with Him.

Ask God to identify a Bible verse or sentence that He is prompting you to embrace and understand.

Reword that Bible verse or sentence into a prayer. Ask God what He wants you to do with it. Write a response to Him about what you sense Him saying. Determine in your heart to live it out.

PART TWO

·····································

How to Hear God Through the Hurt

In the second half of our study, we'll be learning how to hear God, and we'll be practicing the habit of stillness. Expect to spend a shorter amount of time studying and a majority of your daily time in a creative form of listening prayer.

Why Is It So Hard to Hear God When I'm Hurting?

If you want to hear God's voice through the hurt, you must _____ into your _____ and _____ _____ _____.

FOUR WAYS TO WATCH FOR GOD

1. Watching _____.

2. Watching _____.

3. Watching _____.

4. Watching _____.

HOW TO BE STILL

Habit #4: Remember to watch for God's answers.

Answers to the podcast fill-in-the-blanks can be found on page 216.

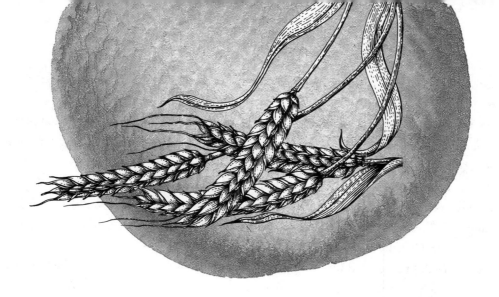

WEEK 4

Remember to Watch

A tiny Christian and Missionary Alliance congregation in Aleppo begins to sing. Language prohibits many from understanding, but the tune to "Christ the Lord is Risen Today" is familiar. *Then a universal word of worship: Ha-a-a-a-a lee-ei-loo-ooo-jah!*[1]

They were no choir of angels. In fact, they should probably not try out for The Voice. So, why did this little video make Fox News?[2]

Because these Christians are singing in the dark for one reason: gathering during daylight may certainly bring death as the Islamic State (most commonly referred to as ISIS) preys on Syrian Christians.

Including believers like Saud.

She'd decided to stop hiding in the dark.

Her city was a blood bath with the torn remains of residents—some her friends and family—blasted onto its walls.[3] But hiding was holding her captive to fear. Together with her husband, she decided that it was time for the family to go back to school and work.

"They will not kill me in my home," she said. "We will live our lives as we always have."[4]

She ended up in a hospital. Her arm nearly gone, and she would never see her husband again this side of heaven.

Doctors had little hope that they could repair the most important asset of her dental practice, her hand. Nearly all of her nerves had been severed. *How will I work? What will I do to feed my children?*

Maybe the hearts of those in war-torn Syria are not that different from those in the seemingly peaceful Western world. Perhaps the circumstances that leave a woman suddenly single don't change the questions dramatically. Parenting alone can be devastating, whether you're a dentist in Syria or a hairdresser in Toledo.

A friend arrived. (Thank God for those faithful ones who rise up to face down the loneliness on our devastating days.) Saud needed to make a decision. Should she have surgery, or not?

"Why? Why? Why?" was all she could mutter from the hospital bed.

"I do not know," said her friend. "But I do know one thing. There is One who sees, listens, and cares. He is with you and waiting to hear one sentence from you: *talk to me, Lord, for I am listening.*"[5]

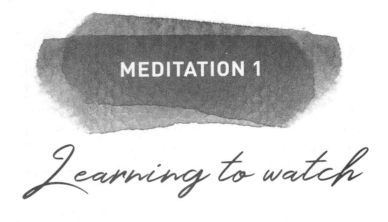

MEDITATION 1

Learning to watch

No, in all these things we are more than conquerors through him who loved us.
(ROMANS 8:37)

God promises we will be conquerors "in all these things."

What things? Losing a husband? An arm? A friend? Your confidence?

Yes. Those things.

Failing in your marriage? Your love life? College? A career?

Yes. Those too.

Even the devastating headlines, wars, and political climate of our nation and world.

The difficult things going on all over the globe are just signs that it's giving birth to the ultimate deliverance. Think about it. If God made Himself a man to live in our world—this world with "these things"—and then died to save us from them . . . is He really going to let them destroy us?

He shows up. The moment we truly need Him, His peace numbs us to the birthing pangs of prophecy. The sweet comfort of God's Spirit dulls us to the clamor of problems in our physical life, but heightens our perception to the things of the spiritual world.

HEARING FROM GOD IS THE ONLY THING CAPABLE OF BIRTHING PEACE BEYOND WHAT WE CAN ASK OR IMAGINE.

That's what Elijah seems to have experienced. He was a man so faithful that the Bible says he did not die but was taken by God.

Imagine a man like that having a pity party.

(I guess we all have them sometimes.)

God had just used the prophet to facilitate one of the greatest and most courageous confrontations of evil in his time. And win. In the exhaustion of the aftermath, spiritual amnesia set in. Elijah forgets his faith and becomes friends with fear. (I guess we all do that too.) He is lying under a bush wishing he was dead when the Angel of the LORD shows up and personally feeds him while he rests. Then, the Rock helps him hide in a cave to sleep a while longer.

God is there, but the weary prophet simply needed *more* of Him. Sometimes we do.

So, the Lord tells him to go outside and stand watch on top of the mountain. Tired as he is, the man pulls himself up and climbs the cliffs. He really wants to see God. Needs to hear Him.

As Elijah watches, a great and powerful wind tore the mountains apart, but the Lord was not in the wind.

Then, the earth quaked. But that's not where God showed Himself.

A fire followed the shaking, but no Sovereign was to be seen.

Finally.

In the stillness.

A gentle whisper.

There. Elijah's eyes could see. His ears could hear.

The great I AM speaks in the silence.

Read Habakkuk 2:1 and write any observations.

Note the two words you previously circled when studying Habakkuk 1:5. Write them below.

What is he looking to see?

Double underline the words watchpost *and* tower. *What do you imagine these structures in Jerusalem would have been used for in the battle-worn ancient world?*

Habakkuk is talking like a soldier in this verse. Both *watchpost* and *tower* would have been built into a fort or the defense wall of a city. The visual picture the prophet paints is of a soldier on duty. Habakkuk is expressing that he is in his army of faith and he will not leave his post. He will stand at attention. In silence. Waiting in *silence* for God's voice.

We need a few more believers who have this mindset in the battle between good and evil, because we are addicted to words. Allergic to silence. We dump our anxiety and frustration at God's doorstep along with a to-do list, and then run off as if He's going to fill our order.

A Syrian theologian who recounted the story of Saud in his reflections on Habakkuk says we pray *at God, rather than talk with* Him. He writes:

> ## *For many of us our prayers are like nasty boys who ring front doorbells and run away before anyone answers.*
> **—DON CARSON**[6]

Habakkuk understands that prayer is a two-way conversation with God. He does not ask his questions without also waiting for an answer. His example cries out to us.

DON'T PLAY DING-DONG DITCH WITH THE GOD OF THE UNIVERSE.

Every single word the Lord has to say is more important than the wisest sentence you'll ever speak. To hear Him, you need to say less and listen more. That requires stillness and silence.

Read Psalm 46:10, where God instructs us to "be still, and know" that He is God. What is the context of this well-known passage? Read the verses before and after it.

Where in this chapter do you see a reference to God's big-picture view of one single problem that is at the root of all of our pain and suffering?

God's command to "be still" is not for people with neat little lives and simple schedules that readily allow for hours on end of contemplation. It's for those of us who are—or feel like we are—in a battle. This psalm was written in reference to an attempted attack on Jerusalem.

What's under attack in your life?

Do you take time to stand watch? To wait for God's answers?

The word *know* in Psalm 46:10 is *yada'*.[7] It is used sometimes to communicate intimacy between a husband and wife. And here it is reminding us we can have that kind of emotional connection with the God of the universe. Whether we're in terrible times or loving a little one through the terrible twos. In spite of hard weeks or bad hair days. How? By turning off Netflix, backing away from our screens, ignoring the din of our electronic calendar, taking our eyes off all the "things," and then waiting for Him to speak.

For many years, I have been growing more mindful of what happens when I just sit with God. I usually do this after I have read my Bible and used my prayer journal. I take time to just be still and listen for His response. Here are a few of the things I've experienced:

- Ideas seem to just pop into my head.
- Energy and motivation are fueled.
- Fear dissolves.
- Peace floods me.
- God directs me to important thoughts and Scripture.
- My love for and intimacy with God grows.

I think that last one is the whole point.

I want you to read it again: love and intimacy with God grows when I sit in stillness with Him.

Let me say it differently: the ultimate experience you can have in your prayer life with God is to be still enough to actually be aware of His presence and let Him direct your thoughts. When you do, you will be undone with love, and you will lose your appetite for all the "things."

THE WORK GOD MOST WANTS US TO SEE IS THE ONE HE IS DOING IN OUR HEARTS.

Underline any of the things in the list on the previous page that you have experienced when you are being still before God. Beside each of these, write a quick summary as you remember how God moved in your heart through stillness.

The Six Habits of Living by Faith

Turn to the back of your book. You'll find the six practices or habits of living by faith that Habakkuk demonstrated. Review that list again.

Here are habits one through four. Circle key words that will help you remember the action you need to take for each of them.

1. Remember to wrestle with God when He seems silent.
2. Remember to look to see where God is at work.
3. Remember to embed questions for God with Truth.
4. Remember to watch for God's answers.

Write the key words or phrases of the first four habits on the following lines.

_____

_____

_____

_____

I have found stillness with God to be an incredibly difficult habit to master. Others have too. C.S. Lewis expressed his frustration with the part of prayer that requires silence. He wrote:

I still think the prayer without words is the best—if one can really achieve it. But I now see that in trying to make it my daily bread I was counting on a greater mental and spiritual strength than I really have. To pray successfully without words one needs to be 'at the top of one's form.'[8]

It seems the stronger I grow in my faith, the more I realize how long it will be until I am at the top of my game. If I ever get there. I have so far to go, but I am still leaning into the habit of stillness. If God says we should do it, I want to experience all He has for me.

Do you?

This week's prayer activities are going to be very different from what you've practiced so far. Hopefully, you have been spending 25–40 minutes on each meditation, with the majority of that time devoted to the study portion. This week, you'll be spending the majority of your time practicing creative listening.

Don't expect a five-step plan. Our different personalities generally require us to listen differently. My man, whom I affectionately call Farmer Bob, hears God clearly when he is on his big tractor mowing the pastures. I tend to hear God best when I'm in a serene and still environment, like when I sit by my fireplace. You'll need to discover what works for you.

Often, when I attempt listening prayer, my to-do list controls my thoughts. So, I take them captive (2 Cor. 10:5). How? I sketch and doodle. Though I am not very good at it, I treasure those drawings. And having busy hands helps me gather my thoughts and tell them: "Hey, you! Get up here in this watchpost with me!" After I am finished sketching, I am often able to be still without need of a prop.

This week, I'd like you to draw whatever thoughts God directs you to in the stillness. Don't know where to begin? Just pick a Bible verse and start to sketch it out.

MEDITATION 2

Watching "perspectively"

Here are a few sentences I overheard when I wrote the first draft of this Bible study.

"They actually ran out of nitro cold brew. It was the worst!"
"We didn't have Wi-Fi all weekend. It was the worst! Ever!"

It's so good to know those things are the worst. Because I thought losing someone you love to cancer might be the worst. Or walking in on a friend who'd committed suicide. I have two friends who have experienced those things, and I'm pretty sure their worst is worse than my worst.

The world gained a little perspective when a novel coronavirus brought us to our knees in prayer.

At the same time, our God is so gentle and understanding. He lovingly meets us in whatever we think is our worst.

It was like that for a sick nine-year-old boy. He was struggling to understand why God would make him stay inside all summer rather than play his beloved baseball. This was his worst. At the time, it was truly devastating.

During his illness, his dad handed him a guitar to give him something to do. That was the musical beginning of one of Christian music's favorite worship leaders: Chris Tomlin. God knew what He was doing. But the musical artist He was making would not be able to see it for many years.[9]

I wonder what God is up to in your life.

We're going to continue to examine Habakkuk 2:1 today. Read it again and see if God brings any new observations to your mind.

Look at the two words you underlined yesterday that reveal where the prophet goes to listen to God. What symbolism can you see in that position? Why is this vantage point going to be helpful?

Habakkuk probably did not go climb into a literal tower, but he figuratively got himself as high as possible because he wanted perspective to see as far as possible. When you're gazing on the proverbial horizon, there are two ways to gaze into the distance: with a perspective of the past and with a perspective of the future. Sometimes it is good to look in both directions.

A PAST PERSPECTIVE

Circle which things God is at work to make good and purposeful in your life according to the verse below.

> And we know that for those who love God all things work together for good, for those who are called according to his purpose.
> (ROM. 8:28)

That may seem basic. It may be unbelievable. But it is true. There is nothing you are facing that God does not see or have intentions to use in your life for good. He doesn't just use glamorous, big, or epic things. He uses *all* things.

One way you can boost your faith for whatever you're facing is to consider the hindsight you now have for a past trial.

Read James 1:2–4 and answer these questions.

What does James tell us to do when we meet trials?

What are the general outcomes of testings?

What does it mean to "count it all joy?" Perhaps it means just that. Count up all the reasons to be thankful right now. You'll find some joy in the making of such a list.

"Thank you that the doctor found that tumor."

"Thank you that dyslexia is making opportunities for me to know my child better."

"Thank you that you've provided the money for me to care for my single adult child while she's sick."

"Thank you that losing my job is helping me see that You alone are my provider."

Anything that makes me need God is a blessing.
—NANCY DEMOSS WOLGEMUTH[10]

I have been using James 1:2–4 to guide me through painful times for fifteen years. I've written many lists of gratitude. It has proven to help me gain perspective, which calms my emotions. I think it will do the same for you.

What is a current suffering that you are facing right now?

Let's apply past perspective to it. In the first column, describe a suffering you faced at some point in your past—big or small. In the second column, list the ways you have seen God's hand in your life as a result of having gone through that circumstance. Then, try to apply that list to things you're facing currently by circling anything in the middle column that is useful to you in your current trial. Finally, in the third column, explain why you circled what you did.

DESCRIBE A PAINFUL TIME FROM YOUR PAST	WRITE A LIST OF HOW THAT TRIAL WAS GOOD FOR YOU	SUMMARIZE WHY YOU CIRCLED SOME OF THE LIST

If only Habakkuk could see what we do about the forthcoming trial his people would face. The hardships ahead were, in part, God's method of bringing His wayward children back to His heart, but a historical perspective allows us to see further. The coming Jewish exile may have helped to set the stage for the good news of Christ's love. Pastor Timothy Keller posits the idea that the exile enabled the faithful remnant of the Hebrew people to introduce the Old Testament to the rest of the world. If they had not been forced out of Jerusalem into other parts of the ancient world, they would not have built synagogues throughout it. The new places of worship became hubs of activity for our first missionaries, such as the apostle Paul.[11]

The exile helped pave the way for Jesus.

What might God be up to in your life or lifetime that will impact generations to come?

A FUTURE PERSPECTIVE

We could benefit from a prescription for our near-sightedness, which shackles us to a selfish perspective limited to what God can do for us in the here and now. God is still at work paving the way for Christ to return a second time and seal the work on the cross, dealing a final blow to death. This matters greatly when we face suffering.

Three of my dearest friends are caring for either their mother or father who suffer with debilitating Alzheimer's disease. One of them, Erin Davis, is finding her comfort as she reframes the way she sees pain by nurturing a perspective vision with her eyes on her Coming King.

She is not belittling the hurt. Her sweet mama, who now requires ongoing help, received the diagnosis with anger and grief. It was a painful several months while her mom resisted the diagnosis in terrible ways.

Until she didn't remember it.

No, Erin is not belittling anything. Instead, she's elevating future hope. This led her to the book of Revelation. It's not usually the book a woman turns to when she's looking for a promise to cling to, but Erin's looking from her *watchpost*. She says: "It's true that God is near the brokenhearted. I need that promise now, but it's not the ultimate promise. Revelation contains ultimate hope."

He will wipe away every tear from their eyes, and death shall be no more, neither shall there be mourning, nor crying, nor pain anymore, for the former things have passed away.
(REV. 21:4)

There, *in end-times prophecy*, Erin is finding the hope she needs to gain perspective on the pain of walking her mom through a devastating disease.

Double underline the words "former things" in Rev. 21:4 on the previous page. What do you think this refers to? Give at least one example of something you are facing right now that could be included under that category.

Erin considers her broken heart *now* a "former thing." That is to say, it's going to be one day. Pain will be erased because it is not eternal.

Pain comes to pass. It does not come to stay.

—ERIN DAVIS[12]

Look up the following Bible verses, which all contain promises to be fulfilled in the end of time. As you read them, listen to God. Let Him bring to mind a current pain you feel which relates to the verse. Then, reword the verse into a future promise from God as it relates to that pain.

	MY CURRENT PAIN:	GOD'S FUTURE PROMISE:
ISAIAH 33:3, 6		
PSALM 72:16		
PSALM 46:9		

We know Habakkuk banked on the bad news about Judah's exile. That is to say, he believed what God said and knew it would come to be. But he also looked beyond it to where it would come to pass. He had future hope.

Some trials are so big that you have to look at them "perspectively." God may not deliver you *from* it, but *through* it as character is formed. And He may be setting the stage for the way He will work in the future, including, but not limited to, His final victory over death when He returns to reign as our King.

Perhaps this seems unrelated to you as you study Habakkuk. Maybe you feel I've detoured because it's hard to understand what the future hope of Christ's return has to do with your current trial or suffering. I guess there have been a few ground-shaking periods of pain in my life wherein I had to know what the end of God's love story with me looked like. Some trials are so big that you have to know the ultimate end game.

Are you looking at your future with Kingdom perspective?

 **Get alone with God again today. Now that you've studied His Word, ask Him to reveal to you what He sees when He looks at your current pain. What perspective does He want you to embrace? Spend time just listening to Him. Use anything He says to guide you as you sketch once again. You're trying to be still. To watch. If He seems to be speaking to you, write down what you sense He is saying. Listen some more. Then, write back to Him. Then, go another round. (Sound sort of like a real conversation? It's supposed to.)**

MEDITATION 3

Watching obediently

After a fight with a friend, all of Kerry Michell's friends rode their bikes home, leaving him behind. He was so lonely on that ride and believes that may have been the day he began to believe the lie that he was not worthy of friendship.

Through his life, he experienced that same feeling often, struggling to fully enjoy the many rich friendships God entrusted to him in his fifty-three years. In the last few weeks of his life, which was cut short by cancer, a friend prayed through that memory with him, and Kerry experienced beautiful freedom as God re-framed the narrative.

But He was not finished with the restoration of this picture.

Kerry's wife Kim wanted his final "ride home" to be full of friends. She texted many of us asking to text photos or videos with a message that said, "Kerry, I'm riding home with you!" It was our honor to send him a photo of my husband Bob with his bike and one of me with one of my horses.

> **There is only one way of victory over the bitterness and rage that comes naturally to us--To will what God wills brings peace.**
>
> **—AMY CARMICHAEL**[13]

A few days later, Kerry went to be with the Lord. Kim invited people to send financial gifts to our True Girl ministry instead of sending flowers in his memory. In my quiet time, I sensed God telling me to use the money to buy bikes for some at-risk boys in the Dominican Republic where we have a team on the ground. My husband, Bob, felt we should buy one for each of Kerry's years on this earth for a total of fifty-three.

During Christmas week, Irving Flete, a coach in a baseball program in the Dominican Republic, and his wife Marlene delivered shiny new bikes to young men and boys who participate in the program. Some of these boys go on to be drafted into major league American baseball teams, but the primary purpose of the program is to reduce fatherlessness by raising up a new generation of godly men. Irving and the other coaches are the only fathers many of the boys ever know. We knew the bikes would be welcomed and helpful to the ministry goals.

This was not on my mind this morning when I was asking God to speak to me and sat in stillness. I was randomly doodling a woodpecker because I'd seen one earlier that morning. But suddenly I had an overwhelming sense that I should "inquire about the fifty-third boy." I knew immediately it was about the last boy who had received a bike.

I texted Marlene to ask if she knew the name of the fifty-third boy.

"Albert" was her confident reply. She followed it up with a photo.

That was fast! I thought. *What is God up to?*

When Irving gave the last group of bikes away, he noticed that one bike was left and looked around to see if they'd missed someone. Albert was standing at a distance, so Irving went to take him the bike. He asked why he was not in the group with the others. The young man explained that he wasn't sure they intended for him to get a bike. Why? Life had beaten him down just hard enough for him to feel unworthy of being in the group with the other boys.

How like Kerry . . .

For some reason, Albert was convinced God did not and could not see him. For that reason, he also did not feel worthy of the bike. Irving promised him that God does see him and that this bike was for him.

My tears began to flow as Marlene recounted the story. I told her, "Tell Albert that God does certainly see him. And to prove it again, he told a woman in Pennsylvania to ask about him!"

I am so thankful that God has trained me to sit in silence to watch and wait for Him to speak. Through the years, I have learned to recognize His voice. I am still learning.

Are you?

We're going to continue to examine Habakkuk 2:1 today because I imagine that we all could use the practice of sitting in our watchtowers. But I have some new things for you to ponder.

Turn to page 46. Review the five qualities of God's voice that you learned from one of the podcasts. Summarize each characteristic in the left column. Then, think of any times you have experienced that quality.

HOW GOD'S VOICE SOUNDS

QUALITY OF HIS VOICE:	MEMORIES OF THAT QUALITY:
1.	
2.	
3.	
4.	
5.	

When God speaks to us, He is not just telling us something we need to hear. He is not just telling us there is something He wants us to do. There is more to it.

Based on John 5:20, what can you surmise God is communicating when He shows us where He is at work and invites us to join Him?

HOW TO TELL GOD YOU LOVE HIM

Look closely at Habakkuk 2:1. Remember, this is military terminology.

Write as many words you can think of to describe how a soldier should behave when awaiting and then receiving the instructions of a superior officer.

Based on John 14:15, what does it say to God when you obey His voice?

Our conversations with God are based on love. The fact that He speaks to us at all *is* love. When we respond obediently to what He says, that is telling Him we love Him too.

Often when God speaks, I'm not sure how He needs me to respond. But even then, I can still be obedient. For example, when I sensed God speaking to me about the boy who got the fifty-third bike, I immediately sought more information. As I did so, it became very clear to me what God was up to. I was able to participate in His work by simply communicating a message of encouragement to Albert through Marlene.

Sometimes it is more difficult. As I shared earlier, I'm deeply burdened for a devastating problem in our nation. Suicide is the second leading cause of death for young people aged 10 to 34.[14] This is the outcome of a growing epidemic of anxiety and depression in those age groups.

When I sensed God asking me to gather an army of mothers and grandmothers to fast for deliverance from anxiety, depression, and suicide, it required some time and planning. Time is a precious commodity to me, as I'm sure it is to you. But obedience to God must always be at the top of my priority list. So I called Sally Burke, the director of Moms In Prayer. I asked if she felt the burden too. She did. And in January of 2020, she and I hosted the first one-hour prayer session to launch what I hope will be a quiet move of God's women concerning this issue.

Sometimes, my obedience involves confessing sin or resolving to be self-controlled because God speaks to me about an area of temptation.

How do you need to obey God right now?

Now that you have been in God's Word, spend as much time as you can just listening to Him. You can begin by sketching, but today's prayer time could take a different turn. When God speaks, respond immediately. If He brings to mind some sin in your life, write a prayer of confession. Then, sit quietly again. Maybe He will bring to mind someone you have not thought of for a long time. Pray for them and then check in with them to see what God might be doing. Respond to Him.

Watching hopefully

For many years, my dream was to be an elementary school teacher. Since I was a young girl, I enjoyed preparing and presenting lessons. (When I was a child I once announced to my family that I would be teaching them a regular Bible study. I even named our little group The Barker Family Fellowship and created a construction paper flag with the letters T.B.F.F.)

When I was older, I put all my heart into any teaching opportunities I could unearth, including volunteering at Sunday school and being a community missionary for Child Evangelism Fellowship.

When I headed off to college, I did not question what my major should be. Elementary education was the obvious choice. (I could not comprehend what all the "undeclared" students were thinking!)

My dream was not meant to be. In a devastating twist, I failed elementary math . . . as a sophomore in college. My advisor had attempted to help, but fractions and division were the death of me. I was encouraged to select another major. (Suddenly, I found myself migrating to the "undeclared" conversations in the cafeteria.)

I could not see then that God was redirecting me to teaching the only thing that would satisfy this Bible-lover's heart. (And not a math problem in sight!) Would I be writing this study right now if my plans had not been interrupted?

Does it seem as if the road map of your life has taken an unexpected twist? Today, I'm passing out invitations for hearts to hope in God's plan.

Look back at Habakkuk 2:2–3 on page 18 to see how God spoke to you when you first examined it.

Draw a little clock above all of the words in Habakkuk 2:2–3 that reference time. What can we expect about how long the prophet might be up in this tower of his?

What (ironically inactive) verb is used in the version below to describe what the prophet will need to do to embrace God's timeline?

> I will climb up to my watchtower
> and stand at my guardpost.
> There I will wait to see what the LORD says
> and how he will answer my complaint.
> **(HAB. 2:1 NLT)**

Read Proverbs 13:12. Record one of the risks of waiting.

In the original Hebrew language, *qal* is the word used when God instructs Habakkuk to "wait" for the vision to come to be. It is an active participle, which is a form of an original verb communicating that the action is continuous and imminent. *Qavah*, which means "to wait," is the original verb. At first glance this may mean absolutely nothing at all. But as a part-time language sleuth, I uncovered something I think you'll want to see.

Qavah comes from the root word *qav*, which means cord. When you pull a cord tightly, it produces a state of tension. (This is beginning to sound like the feeling I have when I'm waiting for God to get around to doing something. You too?)

But here's the thing: *Qavah* is neither the act nor the feeling of the tension, but what happens when that cord finally experiences release. It's a positive word, which suggests that the person doing the active, imminent waiting is experiencing a good sensation. In English, we call that feeling *hope*. In fact, the word *qavah* in all its forms is sometimes translated as "wait," and in other places it is translated as "hope."[15]

Look up the following verses which also use this word or a form of it. What are the writers of these passages of Scripture waiting or hoping for? Write a note beside each, or a collective summary, with any observations you have.

Psalm 25:5

Psalm 27:14

Psalm 39:7

Isaiah 8:17

Lamentations 3:25

Now read James 1:2–4 once again. What does this passage say we will lack in our times of waiting through painful circumstances?

Based on this, what do you think Habakkuk was truly waiting for in his watchpost *or* tower*?*

WAITING FOR PERSPECTIVE

Waiting on God is a major theme in the Bible. The prophets who were often foretelling terrible news used this terminology. They did not mean that they expected God to eventually show up. He was obviously right there, as they were communicating with Him. It also didn't mean they were expecting Him to provide or do things. Rather, waiting seemed to be about what was happening in their hearts in the present, not just what would unfold in their lives in the future. They were waiting for their desires to no longer be directed at the things God could *give them* or *do for them*, but to be transformed into a hope for His presence alone.

We're invited to follow the example of Habakkuk and others who truly *knew* God. Right now—no matter what loss or dying dream is assaulting your heart—you can experience hope.

You can lose everything, and find you lack nothing.

That is not to say you won't experience disappointment, but it can be overridden by a greater sense of what you know to be true of God's character and His promises. That is true hope.

Cross out the definition below that is not consistent with how the Bible uses the word *hope*. Circle the one that seems to be more biblical.

HOPE
(hop)

noun. An optimistic state of mind that is based on an expectation of positive outcomes with respect to events and circumstances in one's life or the world at large.[16]

noun. A confident awareness of God's promises and character that enables me to remain patient and calm in spite of the events and circumstances in my life.

In our Western world we have had a really hard time learning this Truth because most of us only get to practice the habit with First World problems on our minds.

Conflicts with our vacation dates and a family event.

Goals to report for our sales team or our online Whole 30 group.

Lousy reports from the weatherman or our love life.

Disappointment in our stock report or the grip on our golf club.

Many of us have never had a truly devastating event disrupt the noise of our life and invite us to sit in the stillness with God. To ache for His very presence.

But some of our brothers and sisters in Christ, including those in China, have had a lifetime of painful trials.

In December 2019, there was a major effort to collect and imprison people of many religions. *The New York Times* referred to it as "mass organized detentions."[17] Pastor Wang Yi was among the Christians who were taken from their homes. He was sentenced to nine years in jail. Prior to being detained, he wrote this:

> I accept and respect the fact that this Communist regime has been allowed by God to rule temporarily. . . . wicked rulers are the judgment of God on a wicked people, the goal being to urge God's people to repent and turn again toward him. For this reason, I am joyfully willing to submit myself to their enforcement of the law as though submitting to the discipline and training of the Lord.[18]

That sounds like a man who is waiting "perspectively" on God and is cooperating with the Lord's big picture plan. He is mostly concerned with participating in God's plan rather than petitioning God to fulfill his own desires.

I saw that same hopeful perspective as the Chinese church came out of hiding in the early days of the novel coronavirus crisis just weeks after this massive persecution. An unidentified pastor from Wuhan sent a prayer request out to the church at large. It contained wisdom to participate in social distancing and obedience to his government, but laden with desire to share the gospel. He wrote:

...we feel that Christians in our city are not only called to suffer with the people, but we have been called to pray for those who are fearful, and to introduce them to the peace of Christ.

Please pray for the peace of Christ to rule and reign in our hearts, so that we may be a witness to those who are without hope.[19]

Wuhan believers were on the streets giving out masks, food, and water at a time when people needed practical help and were considering their mortality. At the risk of their own health or imprisonment for being exposed as Christians, they went to the streets of Wuhan to offer the hope of the gospel in the midst of terrifying times.

I'm sure these believers love their families dearly. And that they care about their health. But in times of crisis, they remember the promises of God, not the persecution of prison or the threat of a virus.

Half the battle in life is knowing what not to forget and forgetting what doesn't need to be remembered.

—DONNA VANLIERE[20]

Oh, that we would grow up in our faith to be like our Chinese brothers and sisters! I long for the day when my "hope" is not for the things of this world, but in the things of God's Kingdom. I believe listening prayer helps us to get past the noise of this world to hear the call of our true purpose in glorifying God.

And therein lies the tension. The battle of listening prayer is waiting patiently and persistently for the things that don't belong in your mind to be quieted, making room for the things God needs you to remember. When your hope is in God alone, your own faithfulness will flourish.

We'll learn more about that tomorrow.

It's time to listen to Him. Don't let your mind grip thoughts of the things you want from God and the actions you desire for Him to take in your life. Wait patiently as you invite your heart to desire satisfaction in Him alone. Draw symbols of what you are relinquishing to His sovereignty. Draw your tears. Be honest but sit in stillness with God as you practice listening prayer concerning your hopes. Wait patiently.

MEDITATION 5

Watching faithfully

FAST FORWARD TO BABYLON >>>

The day we learned that our son and daughter-in-law were expecting MoMo twins was also the day we departed for some ministry work in South Africa. My heart erupted with double joy at the news, but it was quickly eclipsed when my son, Robby, explained what MoMo meant. The girls were Monoamniotic-Monochorionic. In short, they faced high risk of death or severe disablement by way of cord entanglement, cord compression, or low nutritional flow through the umbilical cord.

The long flight overseas gave us time to look the words high-risk pregnancy in the face. Jet lag invited us to look even longer. Neither Bob nor I slept much that first week.

But we did pray.

And cry.

A lot.

Looking at the problem was becoming a problem.

Sometimes you have to look to what you cannot see.

On a flight between cities, I was in the Johannesburg International Airport where I walked past a baby store. There in the window was the cutest little patchwork sundress with a giraffe ornamenting the skirt.

I did not think long. I marched straight into that store, pointed to the dress in the window and said, "I'll take two."

I decided to live by faith.

I slept better that night.

We're fast-forwarding to Babylon again today. Open your Bible and read Daniel 6:3–22 to gain a quick overview of what we'll study. Jot down any observations you might have as we begin our study today focused on living by faith.

When you hear the story of Daniel in the lion's den, do you envision a young, strong man who likes to eat veggies? Think again. He was old. (Perhaps the word *spry* applies?) He may have grown weak in body, but he had not lost any muscle mass when it came to his conviction.

What did Daniel's career portfolio look like by this, his eightieth year of life?

You do not have to be in "full-time ministry" to serve God fully. Let me stand on my holy soapbox beside Daniel and invite you to dive into any career with a heart to serve the Lord. May every email, phone call, or meeting bring honor to Him (Col. 3:23).

I enjoyed ten years of serving Him as the owner of a secular radio station, community magazine, and marketing agency. The influence I had on the lost was far greater in that career than the one I have now.

Why did Daniel's enemies have to trap him with something that had to do with God's law or the "rules of his religion"? (NLT)

The New Living Translation uses the word faithfully *to describe Daniel's walk. Look back on page 23 to see what definition you wrote for* faith *way back in Week 1, Meditation 2 of our studies.*

Write your definition here: Faith is _____.

We read about three tests of Daniel's faith in this passage. Look at verses 4, 10, and 16. Give each test a "category" under the **Type of Test** *he faced. Then, under* **Daniel** *summarize how he passed that test. (We'll come back to the last column in a few minutes.)*

TYPE OF TEST	DANIEL	YOU
1._____		
2._____		
3._____		

We have a hard time imagining how terrifying this snapshot into Daniel's life may have been because our Sunday school mentality has tamed a wild story.

Earlier we discovered that Habakkuk's reference to things like "fish hooks" was easily verified by archeological finds and ancient documents. I wondered what similar sources might reveal about throwing a grown man into a hole to be eaten by lions.

I could not find anything dating back to Babylon itself, but my research led me to *Damnatio ad bestias*, which is Latin for "condemnation to beasts." It was a form of Roman capital punishment in which a condemned person was killed by wild animals, usually lions or other big cats. It began in ancient Rome about two hundred years before Christ's birth but was rooted in other ancient cultural blood sport. (I can hardly believe I'm referring to it as entertainment.)

Daniel may be one of the only believers in Scripture to face this "sport," but he would not be the last. Hundreds of Christians would be devoured as part of the horrors of halftime at Roman events.

What does that mean for you living in your world today? Let's put you through essentially the tests Daniel faced.

Look back at the three categories you created. Answer the three questions below, and then plot your responses to the corresponding three categories in the previous chart under the word You.

1. If you were accused of being a Christian, would there be evidence to prove it? If yes, what would that evidence be? If no, what is lacking?

2. *When your faith is put on trial by social trends and government laws, do you obey God no matter what it might cost you? If so, how? If not, why?*

3. *The last time you faced something truly fearful, did you walk through it with the kind of faith that others recognized and spoke of? Write about your response to that test below.*

LION'S DEN DAZE

Daniel had every right to be afraid of praying in public when the king wrote an edict that targeted the beliefs of faithful Jews. And he could have chosen to be terrified out of his mind when he faced the lion's den. But he risked his life rather than deny his God. He chose faith.

The faith that Daniel and our brothers and sisters in China embrace is not ultimately in God rescuing them *from* their "lion's den", but *through* it to glorify God. Like Jesus, they did not want the suffering but willingly submitted to the will of the Heavenly Father rather than invoke their own (Luke 22:42). Their faith is wrapped in heavenly perspective, obedience, and hope.

I'm working on being that kind of Christian. I want to desire and submit to His will and not my own. I long to have a faith that is truly rooted in the conviction that God's plan—whatever it may look like—is the best path for my life.

> *Would you like to have the story of Daniel without the lion's den? Of course, we wouldn't because we know the end of the story. Well, we Christians, we've got this whole book full of wonderful stories like that and the end of every single one of them is the same. It's glory every time.*
>
> **—ELISABETH ELLIOT**[21]

When my daughter-in-law's pregnancy was labeled high-risk by doctors, anxiety and sleep-lessness tried to devour me. When they came together, I called them "the anaconda" in my journal. I began to note how often I mentioned it on my pages of prayer.

I resolved to stop feeding the anaconda. Instead, I fed my faith with Scripture and began recording that in my journal. My entries progressed from pleadings for God to save our sweet babies to surrender that His will be done.

When I got to delivery week, it was worse than I wanted it to be—one of the twins, Addie, suffered a collapsed lung within twenty-four hours of their premature arrival—but God was more than I needed Him to be. I continued to record the Truth:

> A mighty fortress. Sacred refuge. Your kingdom is unshakable. You are a consuming fire. "The sheep need not be terrified by the world; they have but to stay close to the shepherd. It is not the praying sheep that Satan fears but the presence of the Shepherd." A.W. Tozer
>
> The miracle of their arrival is [that there is] no entanglement in their umbilical cords. This is very uncommon [for MoMo twins], and a sweet gift from the Lord. Addie has a collapsed lung and we are not seeing dramatic improvement. Father, you created Addie & Zoe. You knit them together in their mother's womb. You kept them full of nutrients and did not allow their cords to entangle or compress. Now, finish what you began strong, sovereign, good Father. Do what you've done again and again.

I don't know what "lion's den" you are facing. You may be trying to stay above the waters of doubt. Whatever it is, let's submit to the kind of faith that yearns for Christ and His glory. Walk in faith, my friend.

For today's prayer activity, you'll spend one last time sitting in stillness. Then, begin to draw symbols of your own current "lion's den" as you listen to Him for directions on how you should walk out your faith.

As you practiced the habit of listening to God this week, your meditation skills have been strengthened. Ask God's Spirit to direct your mind and heart to what He intends for you to embrace from this week's meditation.

- *Ask God to identify a Bible verse or sentence that He is prompting you to embrace and understand.*

- *Reword that Bible verse or sentence into a prayer. Ask God what He wants you to do with it. Write a response to Him about what you sense Him saying. Determine in your heart to live it out.*

What's the Right Kind of Fear?

1. Our call to live in _____ is first introduced to us in _____ to _____.

2. _____ is the _____ of _____. You cannot _____ in the way of something if you're _____ in the _____ direction.

3. We want to be _____ rather than _____, we must enter into ongoing _____ _____.

TWO KINDS OF PRIDE

1. _____

2. _____

TWO KINDS OF PRIDE

BELITTLING ————————————————————— BOASTING

Habit #5: Remember to fear God.

Answers to the podcast fill-in-the-blanks can be found on page 216.

WEEK 5

Remember to Fear

Legalism had strangled the passion out of the church on the Scottish Hebrides Islands. The congregations were emptying. Most of the remaining believers were old. Many had a bad case of spiritual amnesia.

But two sisters in their 80s—one blind and the other bent with arthritis—had been pleading with God to bring revival. From 10 p.m. until 3 a.m., Peggy and Christine Smith prayed and began to sense God was promising something. That is what they sensed when they came to Isaiah 44:3, which reads: "I will pour water on the thirsty land, and streams on the dry ground."

They told their pastor. He petitioned other leaders and together they wrote a resolution to "turn again unto the Lord whom we have so grieved with our waywardness and iniquities" and to pray that the villages would be "visited with a spirit of repentance."[1] People began to gather to pray in a barn two evenings a week, while the sisters continued prayer in their cottage.

Several weeks later, during the 3 a.m. hour in a barn, one young man stopped praying for the Island. And started seeing his own need.

"God, are my hands clean? Is my heart pure?"[2]

It was the right question. Immediately, the presence of God gripped every person present. The group of intercessors left to find men and women kneeling along the roads, crying out to God. Every home had lights on. No one could sleep with the awareness of God's presence overwhelming them.

For three years, widespread revival swept through the Scottish islands.[3]

MEDITATION 1

Pride comes before a fall

FAST FORWARD TO BABYLON »»

Everything in me wants to pull out some pages from the story in the vault of my memory right now. Chapters that make me the martyr. And tales that talk of nameless—though identifiable to some—individuals as the villains of those pages of my life.

(Sigh.)

But I'm going to take the high road and simply tell you this: God has used completely lost individuals who were deeply mired in their own sin to confront me in mine. The fact that God used someone "worse" than me became the packaging on a gift I needed very much: to be reminded to walk in humility.

If someone "more evil" than you has "won" in the game of life at your expense, I have two things to share with you.

First, open your Bible to Psalm 7. I have worn it out a few times as I wrestle with God about relationships gone awry. It will get you through. Second, hear this important life lesson from Habakkuk: sometimes God uses those who are the epitome of pride to help us see our own.

Let's let God help us see what we might prefer to be blind to.

 **This week we're examining a swath of Scripture where God describes the Babylonians and their five significant sinful characteristics. Today we will discover and explore the root of all those flaws: pride. Read Habakkuk 2:4. Record any observations you have.**

Who is "puffed up," and what might that mean?

This power-packed verse implies something about the Babylonians. It's unstated, but God is going to allow their pride to be their downfall. If walking righteously in faith brings life, we can assume walking pridefully brings death. This verse is the beginning of a big can of "woe" for Babylon.

PRIDE COMES BEFORE A FALL

Put your finger in the book of Habakkuk, as we fast forward to the first glimmer of God's judgment on the enemy of His people. As we travel through time, picture Babylon rising out of the desert plains like New York City with its forest of skyscrapers. The empire is an uncontested world power. And its king, Nebuchadnezzar, has no peers. It's easy to see how a guy like that might become the poster child for pride.

Read Daniel 4:28–37. Answer these questions:

How did King Nebuchadnezzar's pride manifest?

What did he hear even before his prideful words were out of his mouth? Describe what was forecasted and immediately came to be for this pompous poo-bah?

Did Nebuchadnezzar really crawl around on all fours and eat grass? Could his hair have grown like feathers and his nails like the claws of animals? It's hard to believe. But, it's possible. Boanthropy is the name of a "psychological disorder in which a human believes himself or herself to be a bovine."[4] (And by that, I mean a cow, buffalo, or bison.) I've never seen it myself, but they say it's certifiable!

Read Proverbs 16:18 and 1 Peter 5:5–6. Explain why Nebuchadnezzar's problem wasn't mental illness, but God's intervention.

Read Daniel 4:34. What did King Nebuchadnezzar remember to do after reason returned to him?

What does Daniel 4:37 tell us that Nebuchadnezzar concluded about walking in pride?

Look at Habakkuk 2:4 one more time. How might it be significant that "the righteous shall live by his faith" is first introduced to us in contrast to pride?

Look back at page 23 where you wrote a definition of faith. *Re-write it below. Then, fill in the blank.*

The object of my faith must be _____.

Now, look at the Oxford Dictionary *definition of pride below and circle the words in this definition that emphasize the object of pride.*

PRIDE

(prid)

noun. A feeling or deep pleasure or satisfaction derived from one's own achievements, the achievements of those with whom one is closely associated, or from qualities or possessions that are widely admired.[5]

A prideful person is all about me, myself, and I. We're talking self-absorption to the extreme.

Read 2 Timothy 3:1–2. This verse describes the condition of the Church in the "last days" before Christ returns. What is one sign that He is coming soon?

TIME FOR TIMELINES!
Turn to pages 222–223 in the back of the book.

Find a spot just left of the high prophetic peak of Christ's second coming to earth. Write: "The Church will overflow with Self-Love."

Let's not be lovers of self who have to be humbled like Nebuchadnezzar. Instead, let's try to humble ourselves before God has to do it for us.

GETTING HUMBLE BEFORE YOU'RE HUMBL**ED**

You'll note that I underlined the last two letters in the word *humbled*. Not only have I learned that humility is an action I have to choose, but also that God will help me if I forget to make the right choice.

I knew ten months ago I could not handle everything coming my way, but I did it anyway. I did it all. And I didn't ask for help. Suffice it to say, my heart was slipping dreadfully close to thinking like Nebuchadnezzar. Anytime we think "it" all depends on us, we reveal the belief that we're the ones who built "it."

About that time, my friend and church elder Andy Mylin preached a message on Psalm 23. He pointed out that God "makes" us lie down in green pastures. Then he said, "sometimes God puts us on our back because we need to look up and see Him."[6]

My spirit stood at attention as if he'd said that sentence just for me.

But I didn't do anything about it.

On Labor Day, I found myself in the ER flat on my back unable to move. (I'm fairly thankful that God chose a herniated disc rather than boanthropy!) God's kindness led me to repentance (Rom. 2:4).

Have you ever felt God was disciplining you like that? Describe that time below.

Wouldn't it be better if you and I never had to be humbled by discipline again because we had so much reverence and respect for God that we hated evil?

This week, I invite you to enter into another fearless inventory of your own life. Begin by praying this out loud each day:

> Search me, O God, and know my heart!
> Try me and know my thoughts!
> And see if there be any grievous way in me,
>   and lead me in the way everlasting!
> (PS. 139:23–24)

For today's prayer activity, you're going to continue practicing stillness. Before you write a prayer below to God, I'd like you to lay down and look up. Just spend some time on your back reminding yourself that you did not create this world—not even your corner of it—and it will go on without you. As you lay in stillness, let God "search your heart" to see if there are symptoms and patterns of pride in your life. Humble yourself.

MEDITATION 2

The right kind of fear

Recent studies reveal that self-obsession is increasing in modern societies to the point of it being referred to as a "narcissism epidemic."[7] Have you ever met a narcissist? I bet you have. They're the ones who—

- feel entitled to the best seat, best car, and best office.
- need to have the silence filled with words and prefer the sound of their own voice.
- can't be quiet enough to hear what others have to say.
- require constant and excessive affirmation.
- are preoccupied with fantasies about their success, power, beauty, or brilliance.
- never ask about the dreams of others.
- exaggerate their achievements and talents and cannot stop telling you about them!
- think their opinion must be plastered all over social media for the good of the world!
- take advantage of others to get ahead.

It's easy to misread a narcissist. They're often the life of the party, so you might mistakenly think they care about you since they are so entertaining. But hang out with them ten times and you'll quickly see that it's actually you that's entertaining their deep need for attention.

The irony is that in spite of all their self-love, they're struggling deeply with self-hatred.

Please let me be a true friend today by helping you examine your own heart. I mean, you'd want me to tell you if you had lipstick on your teeth, right? Well, nothing could be worse than wearing the smudge of narcissism to a party and being the last to know.

Warning: brave soul searching straight ahead.

Read Habakkuk 2:5, keeping in mind that this is still revealing God's thoughts about the Babylonians. Record any observations you have.

Circle the word in today's passage that's synonymous with pride.

Underline all the words that reveal the outcome of pride.

Look back at the inventory you completed on living in faith or fear. It's on pages 25–28. Jot down any glaring concerns God revealed to you.

Review the two types of pride from this week's podcast. Draw them on a continuum below.

> *The Christian Gospel is that I am so flawed that Jesus had to die for me, yet I am so loved and valued that Jesus was glad to die for me. This leads to deep humility and deep confidence at the same time. It undermines both swaggering and sniveling. I cannot feel superior to anyone, and yet I have nothing to prove to anyone. I do not think more of myself or less of myself. Instead, I think of myself less.*

—TIM KELLER[8]

The goal of the quiet life of every believer must be that our thoughts are so consumed by God and His Truth that we grow a deep taproot of faith. Like a tree planted by water, we find everything we need from beneath the surface and are unbothered by the tugging. This frees us from the badgering thoughts of our self and lets us become a shelter for others as we stand calmly in confident humility. We don't lean toward either of pride's forms, but dwell in faith and (here's the key) the right kind of fear.

Look up Proverbs 8:13. What's the right kind of fear?

FEAR OF GOD	To bow before, to worship, to submit to, to stand in awe of God.[9]

When we bow before God and worship Him, it fosters our love relationship, and our sense of His awesome power grows. This facilitates a desire to submit to Him in all things, which erases our obsession with ourselves but bolsters our sense of true value in Christ. The end result is that the fear of this world fades. Our faith is fueled to a place where the only thing to fear is God Himself. And that is not a fearful thing, at all. He is good.

The Six Habits of Living by Faith

Turn to the back of your book. You'll find the six practices or habits of living by faith that Habakkuk demonstrated. Review that list again.

Here are habits one through five. Circle key words that will help you remember the action you need to take for each of them.

1. **Remember to wrestle with God when He seems silent.**
2. **Remember to look to see where God is at work.**
3. **Remember to embed questions for God with Truth.**
4. **Remember to watch for God's answers.**
5. **Remember to fear God.**

Write the key words or phrases of these five habits on the following lines.

_____

_____

_____

_____

_____

Someone once said, "A word of caution but profound truth to the alcoholic man and woman wanting to recover more than just drying out: 'You cannot solve a problem on the same level of mind that created it.'"[10] We too will not sober up from our pride unless we let another mind solve the problem.

This week, our task is to let our thoughts be taken captive by the One who truly can set us free from the bondage of our sin. Let's submit willingly to God as He searches our hearts.

Today, we'll be even braver in the fearless inventory of our hearts. Remember to begin by praying this out loud:

> Search me, O God, and know my heart!
>   Try me and know my thoughts!
> And see if there be any grievous way in me,
>   and lead me in the way everlasting!
> (PS. 139:23–24)

Let God "search your heart" to see if there are symptoms and patterns of pride in your life. Take time to prayerfully consider each of these ways that pride manifests.

PRIDE BY BOASTING

Check any of the ways below that you're guilty of practicing pride in the form of boasting.

_____You have no ability to say "no" because you think everyone needs you. You believe the lie that nothing can be done without you.

_____You collect people and build relationships for the sole purpose of achieving your personal and professional goals. (Phil. 2:1–3)

_____You're annoyed by the needs of others and feel inconvenienced when you are required to help them. (Phil. 2:4)

_____You expect the best seat in the house, at the restaurant, in an airplane. (Matt. 20:16)

_____You talk about yourself. A lot. And you like to let people know about your accomplishments and titles. (Prov. 27:2)

_____You struggle with lying, which often comes in the form of exaggeration. (Ps. 31:18; 59:12)

_____You rarely, if ever, take time to give credit to God for your achievements and gifts. (1 Cor. 1:31; James 1:17)

_____You've stopped seeking God with all your heart, mind, and soul because you've forgotten how much you need Him. (Ps. 10:4)

_____You default to criticizing others and pointing out their faults, but you rarely are conscious of your own spiritual sin. (Rom. 2:1–3) You hide your weaknesses. (2 Cor. 12:9)

_____You believe that your position negates the need for you to confess sin to others who can help you. (James 5:16; Prov. 28:13)

PRIDE BY BELITTLING

Check any of the ways below that you're guilty of practicing pride in the form of belittling.

_____You don't ask for help because you don't want to be a bother. You try to do everything on your own. (2 Cor. 3:5; Gal. 6:2)

_____You worry about what people think of you. In fact, you waste a lot of time fearing what their thoughts might be. (Prov. 29:25)

_____You're easily hurt if your accomplishments and work are not noticed, or if others are praised. (James 3:14–16)

_____You cannot stop thinking about your sin and feel highly condemned, as opposed to convicted. (Rom. 8:1)

_____You're unnaturally withdrawn from others and excuse it as introversion or shyness. You don't share your thoughts about God because you're afraid of what people will think of you. (1 Peter 3:15)

_____You're prone to a works-based salvation, worrying that you're not doing enough to be a good Christian rather than resting in the finished work of Jesus on the cross. (Acts 15:10)

_____You avoid trying new things or going into certain social settings because you are paralyzed by fear of failure. (2 Tim. 1:7)

_____Many hours in your day are bogged down by anxiety. You may be a perfectionist to the point of frustrating yourself and others because of your fears. (Phil. 4:6–7)

_____You feel like the weak link or black sheep of the family or friend group. You struggle to see how you could contribute at church. (1 Cor. 12)

_____You're self-conscious of your appearance, having to approve photos before they're posted online or hiding behind others in group photos. (Ps. 139:14)

Now write a prayer to God based on what He reveals to you.

_____

_____

_____

_____

_____

_____

_____

MEDITATION 3

Facing greed and materialism

If I could lift your chin and invite your eyes to look into mine right now, I would do it. And I would promise you that though this week's work is not comfortable, it assures revival.

If ever we need God to show up to revive us, it is when our spirits are wilted by worry or downcast by devastations.[11] I have known that kind of rescue many times in my walk with Jesus, and it is my great joy to lead you toward the possibility of experiencing it this week.

In a book titled *Brokenness*, Nancy DeMoss Wolgemuth asks the question: what kind of heart does God revive? She answers it with this verse:

> For thus says the High and Lofty One
> Who inhabits eternity, whose name is Holy:
> "I dwell in the high and holy place,
> with him who has a contrite and humble spirit,
> to revive the spirit of the humble,
> and to revive the hearts of the contrite one."
> (ISA. 57:15 NKJV)

Habakkuk does not approach God only to wrestle and wait, but to humble himself and confess. He's seeking revival.

Read Habakkuk 2:6–11. Today we will examine the greed and materialism of the Babylonians. Record any observations you have.

Circle the word him *each time it occurs. To whom do you think this is referring?*

Every time we see the word *him*, it's referring to the specific enemy of Judah, Babylon. But who is God giving these words to? Habakkuk and the rest of the Hebrews. These words are for them. But they're for the *hers* too. God is burdened by anyone who participates in the same kinds of things. Let our hearts be poised to enter into the work of humble contrition today.

Put a square around the word woe *each time it occurs.*

WOE
(woe)

noun. 1.) a condition of deep suffering from misfortune, affliction, or grief; 2.) ruinous trouble: CALAMITY, AFFLICTION.[12]

A woe is either an emotion or the cause of it. Based on the definition above, who do you think is feeling the emotion, and who do you think is causing it in the passage we're studying?

In your Bible, draw brackets around the two woes we'll explore today. Label them Woe #1: Greed *and* Woe #2: Materialism.

Specifically, what does Habakkuk 2:6 tell us the Babylonians heaped up?

The book of Habakkuk has been dubbed "little Job" by some theologians. In that book of the Bible, Satan accused Job of only loving God for all that was given to him. Satan sought permission from God to take this good man's things away to prove it. God said yes.

Read Job 1:17. Who did Satan use to plunder Job?

Job was faithful even after he lost his fortune, family, and friends to the selfish greed of a young but tyrannical nation. But I think Satan was right about most of us. It's easy to become a Christian who treats God like a genie in a bottle who exists supremely to fulfill our every wish.

When our prayer time lacks the habit of listening to God, we quickly default to master of our own universe.

Find 2 Timothy 3:2–4 again. Right after Paul states that people will be lovers of self, he gives another characteristic of the church in the final days before Christ's return. Write it below.

Flip over to 1 Timothy 6:6–12 and answer these questions.

What two things does Paul write about in verse 8 that should be enough to make us content? Do you have those things? If so, are you content or do you want more?

What is a possible risk of craving things and amassing debt according to verses 7 and 10?

How is debt like theft?

According to verse 11, what six things should we pursue instead of stuff?

Circle the one that he gives special attention to in verse 12. Why?

The love of money is in contrast to living in faith. It proves we are afraid that God cannot or will not provide enough and that we are not satisfied in Him. We have forgotten that He is enough.

> ### *Covetousness is desiring something so much that you lose your contentment in God. The opposite of covetousness is contentment in God.*
> **—JOHN PIPER**[13]

Do you have contentment in God? Or do you believe you'll find it when you buy that "one more thing"?

It seems there are a lot of "one more things" that cause me to wrestle with materialism and greed. Right now, I really crave a black and white gingham fleece throw. I've been pondering the purchase for a few weeks now. It's on sale for $39. How beautifully it would break up the color of my red sectional and pull in my new carpet—the one I "needed" to buy last month to make a larger, softer crawl space for the grandbabies!

I don't know if it's right or wrong for me to have this blanket, but my heart has been wrestling with it. The very fact that I'm gripped with questions is both healthy and alarming. It proves God is speaking to me and inviting me to talk to Him about the things I buy and the way I use His money. That's the good news. It also proves that my appetite for things is alive and well. That's the bad news.

I'd rather have an abundant life with the ratty old yellow cotton throw that's on my lap right now, than risk wandering from the faith over a purchase I probably won't remember in a few years. Maybe you think that sounds ridiculous, but here's something I've learned.

EVERY DECISION—NO MATTER HOW SMALL—EITHER GIRDS OUR MEMORY WITH FAITH OR DULLS IT WITH FEAR.

Listen to God specifically concerning the issues of greed and materialism as we continue a fearless inventory of our hearts. Remember to begin by praying this out loud:

Search me, O God, and know my heart!
    Try me and know my thoughts!
And see if there be any grievous way in me,
    and lead me in the way everlasting!
(PS. 139:23–24)

For today's prayer activity, go for a brisk walk outside. (Even if it's cold! I walk my dog in twenty-degree Pennsylvania winters. You can do this.) My intention is to get you away from your things. Notice God's beautiful world. His creation. As you walk, be mindful of birds, tree trunks, sky color, and anything else He illuminates. Say "thank you" out loud to Him when you see something you're grateful for.

Don't ignore the content of our study time. As you settle into His gift of creation, invite Him to talk to you about your material items. Respond in obedience if you hear something from Him.

MEDITATION 4

Facing abuse of human life and exploitation

Napoleon is my breathtaking friend.

He's an Indian peacock who hatched right here on my farm. (His father was Alexander the Gresh.)

In May, when his feathers are at their peak, there are few things more beautiful than seeing him strut with his tail spread proudly. (An ironic word to use when we're trying to dig down deep to find our "humble" this week!)

A couple of weeks ago, Napoleon wasn't feeling well. He was gaping. When a bird begins to stretch its neck and open its mouth often, that's usually a sign that gapeworms have taken up residence in its throat. Left untreated, it's just a matter of time before the long-lasting curse on our world claims another beauty. The bird doesn't go quietly but suffocates slowly.

Not on my watch.

With the help of Farmer Bob, I isolated our patient and began to treat him. But a week later, he was beginning to rasp. His breathing was becoming labored.

This may sound crazy to you, but I pray over my animals. And when they are sick, I touch them and pray in the name of Jesus. I pray as if it all depends on heaven, and I act as if it all depends on me. On this particular day, that meant increasing a dose of medication I was giving him.

Yesterday, our grand boy was walking the farm again.

What a fulfilling sight.

God created us, and then invited us to take care of the rest of His creation (Gen. 1:28).

You don't have to love animals like I do, but when you stand before Him one day, will you be able to say you were a faithful steward of all of His creation?

Read Habakkuk 2:12–17. Today we will examine Babylon's reputation for exploitation and abuse. Record any observations you have.

Put a square around the word woe *each time it occurs.*

Bracket off each of the following two categories. Which verses do you feel speak to the abuse of human life and which are about exploitation? Label them Woe #3: Abuse of Human Life *and* Woe #4: Exploitation.

Use the chart below to record any manner in which you see abuse of life and exploitation in ancient Babylon or today's world. I'll prompt you to come back to this chart a few times. For now, focus on what you see in verses 12–17. Write each example on a line under the correct category.

BABYLON'S ABUSE OF HUMAN LIFE & EXPLOITATION	MODERN ABUSE OF HUMAN LIFE & EXPLOITATION

Double underline the four additional things that Babylon exploited as mentioned in verse 17. Write them under their category.

Those who wield their power to abuse other people, animals, and the earth are a great source of grief to God. Unfortunately, the exploitative mentality did not die with the destruction of Babylon. Let's look at each of them and consider how these abuses and exploitations are alive and well today.

MURDER

Babylon was known for bloody battles that killed innocent people. Its famous Code of Hammurabi listed punishments for crimes that included cutting out someone's tongue, eye, ear, hands, or breasts.[14] There's one thing Babylon was not guilty of, though common during the era: human sacrifice.

Look back at page 37. Who was guilty of worshipping Molech, a god that required child sacrifice?

Despite occasional efforts by godly kings, worship of Molech wasn't abolished until the Israelites' captivity in Babylon. (Hmmm? Can you say "humbled"?)

How does our culture shed innocent blood? Write them on one corresponding line under "Modern Abuse of Human Life & Exploitation."

SEXUAL ABUSE

The imagery of verse 15 (making a neighbor drunk to take advantage of them) is agreed to be a metaphor for the way Babylon seduced neighboring nations with their power and then pillaged them when they were "drunk." God's message is that both nations and individuals who devalue life in this way deserve punishment. Babylon was guilty of both. Its polytheistic gods *loved* sex. And lots of it. Therefore, females were often victimized as child temple prostitutes, and every one of them was expected to spend one night in a temple where she had to have sex with any man of any age who was the first to place a coin in her lap.

The Bible is full of the raw and real stories of abuse against women during Old Testament times. It is natural that this would trouble you. It troubles God too.

Women suffer the effects of sin when culture decays. In fact, the treatment of women can be seen as a barometer of a nation's relationship with God.

—PROFESSOR CHRIS MILLER, CEDARVILLE UNIVERSITY

When you come to a story of a woman being abused in the Bible, I encourage you to read the full context. They were often avenged by godly men. Wars often broke out when just one woman was abused. Good men fought for those women.

How do you see sexual abuse in our culture today?

And there are good men and women still fighting for those who need to borrow courage. You may be a victim of the tyrannical power of someone. It's my prayer that you'll tell someone. There is healing for you. God is grieved and angered by what was done to you. And there are safe, good people who can help you heal.

Add "sexual abuse," and anything else you can think of that applies, on one corresponding line under "Modern Abuse of Human Life & Exploitation" in the chart.

DESTRUCTION TO THE EARTH

The majestic cedar tree forest of Lebanon, which is mentioned in today's passage, is considered a vanished forest. During Habakkuk's day, this graceful shelter would have covered the mountains of the eastern Mediterranean region and was likely an authentic Animal Kingdom that would have put Disney's to shame. The cedars were used to build the temple in Jerusalem. They're a slow-growing variety with a reputation for a wood that's all but indestructible. The Babylonians stripped the forest.

Why do you think Babylon was eager to cut those trees down? What would they have been used for?

How does our culture destroy this earth? Write them on one corresponding line under "Modern Abuse of Human Life & Exploitation."

ABUSE OF ANIMALS

We've covered the fact that I want to meet Mrs. Noah one day, and you know I am an animal lover. Did you know I currently care for about nineteen pets? Horses, llamas, fainting goats, a very fat mini-donkey, three beautiful peacocks, and a beloved labradoodle named Moose have my heart! So, you know I searched high and low to see if God was concerned about animal abuse in Babylon. I came up empty. But let me draw some logical conclusions.

I immediately thought of Daniel and the lion's den. What we know of *Damnatio ad bestias*[15] in Rome is that the big cats were starved so that they would put on a bloody show. This would have been abusive.

It could also refer to the fact that the destruction of the forest left animals homeless and vulnerable, or that the destruction of neighboring nations included the senseless slaughtering of animals.

Look up Proverbs 12:10 and Psalm 145:9. What can you conclude about how God wants us to care for animals?

How do you see animal cruelty in your corner of the world? Write it on one corresponding line under "Modern Abuse of Human Life & Exploitation."

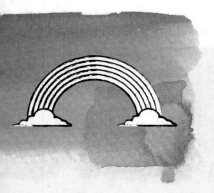

THE CITIES

You've been reading covenant language in today's passage. Verses 14 and 16, which foretell the downfall of Babylon, are full of it.

Let's first examine verse 16. Circle the words uncircumcision *and* cup. *How might the use of these be covenant language?*

Babylon, who has exposed the nakedness of many, will soon feel the thirst from the hot desert air. And in that state of full revelation, there will be no evidence of covenant circumcision on the foreskin of every male as would be true of the Jewish people.

Now compare verse 14 to Isaiah 11:9. What's similar in these two passages?

This reference to Isaiah's writing "raises the oracle from a single reference to Babylon's defeat and places it on the level of eschatology."[16] There is coming a day when God will inflict judgment on the most powerful worldly empire and it will be destroyed, but more importantly, He has good plans for Judah.

Read Isaiah 2:1–5. Describe God's ultimate plan.

In Habakkuk 2:17, God expresses anger that Babylon has done violence to "the cities and all who dwell in them." This is a differentiation from and in addition to violence that caused "the blood of man." He's not just concerned with murder to individuals but something more. It's not only that the Babylonians are the bullies on the ancient Middle East's proverbial block. The reference to "cities" is pointing out that they've raised their hands against the holy homes of God's chosen people.

Let me remind you that God is expressing His anger to the point of promising the destruction of Babylon for participating in these atrocities.

I'd like to think that we don't have to "take inventory" of ourselves on these topics. But a brave moral inventory looks under every rock in our hearts.

How might all of these "woes" that grieve God be rooted in pride?

Today, we examined some pretty heavy and heady stuff. But even the painful and difficult topics are important. Ask God to help you absorb what He needs you to embrace. Remember to begin by praying this out loud:

Search me, O God, and know my heart!
　　Try me and know my thoughts!
And see if there be any grievous way in me,
　　and lead me in the way everlasting!
(PS. 139:23–24)

For today's prayer I want you to sketch again. Are there any of the categories we have considered today that have not been of concern to you? Select something of beauty from that topic and draw it worshipfully. You might draw a great tree or a peacock. Maybe you'll sketch out babies crawling or beautiful women worthy of respect. Pause to consider if God would like you to demonstrate stronger stewardship in any of the categories.

MEDITATION 5

Facing idolization of image

FAST FORWARD TO BABYLON >>>

On my desk sit five enormous study Bibles. They've gotten a workout these past several months as I wrote this study. (What will take you six weeks, took me six months.) The Bibles are held up by two natural agate bookends. Both are solid mineral rock that grow with age.

Bookends are powerful things. They hold stuff in place.

Habakkuk uses two bookends in his poem.

One is pride. (We find it at the front end of the woes.) And the other is idolatry. (We find it here at the end of the woes.) Both are made of solid stubborn worship of creature rather than Creator and grow over time.

And they both hold up the stuff that's between them—greed, materialism, abuse of human life, and exploitation.

Sometimes you should not keep your bookends.

Today we will examine the final woe, idolatry of the Babylonians. Read Habakkuk 2:18–20 and record any observations you have.

Put a square around the word woe. *Let's recall what it means. Write it below.*

Bracket off this woe as you have the others and write Woe #5: Idolatry *beside it.*

Circle all the references in the passage concerning an idol's ability to speak and communicate with us. How many are there? Why do you think this is the emphasis?

This is not Habakkuk's first mention of idolatry or lesser gods. Look at 1:11. What does this verse say Babylon had set up as an idol?

WORSHIPPING MUTE IDOLS

Put your finger in the book of Habakkuk again. It's time to travel forward to Babylon. King Nebuchadnezzar has been building something new for his magnificent city.

Read Daniel 3:1–7. Answer these questions:

How tall was the statue Nebuchadnezzar made?

Why would he have built such an idol? (You might look back at chapter 2.)

Who participated in the worship of this idol?

What was used to signal worship of the idol? How does this support Habakkuk's references to an idol's inability to speak?

It seems Nebuchadnezzar wanted to streamline worship. Perhaps the many gods were getting too demanding. Or maybe the king really did dig Daniel's God as stated in Daniel 2:47, but he didn't understand Him. Some scholars think the ruler just forgot about the One True God and had a statue of himself built. That would not be a far stretch. If Babylonian culture had anything trademarked, it was image management.

Idolatry may seem like a sin that women of the new millennium don't fall prey to, but it goes way beyond bowing down to gold statues. It's essentially trusting in anything man-made. Anything *we've* made. It's trusting in our own power as creators and sustainers.

Of our careers.

Our talents.

Our money.

Our families.

Our friendships.

Our churches.

And ultimately our image.

Circle any of the things above that might be idols in your life. Use the space above to add anything else that comes to mind.

Friend, I've got to ask something that very well could be just for me. Take it or leave it. But if it stings, it's probably for both of us. Is it possible that our obsession with selfies is just a modern version of setting up an image for self-worship?

I'm troubled. I've travelled to some beautiful places in this world of ours and have seen some amazing things. How is it that when I arrive at Victoria Falls or I'm swimming with a great sea turtle that I think: *I should take a picture of* **ME?!**

I'm vain. I have good hair days. I have bad ones. (When I'm in the Dominican Republic, the humidity ensures that they will be very bad.) Why do I only post the images of me that sparkle . . . like gold?

AS WE ESCALATE IN OUR PRIDE AND IMAGE MANAGEMENT, WE BEGIN TO READ THE BIBLE THROUGH THE LENS OF OURSELVES. THIS MUTES THE VOICE OF SCRIPTURE IN OUR HEARTS, AND WE CANNOT HEAR WHAT IT IS SAYING TO US.

You will never receive the revival you need as long as you are consumed with the idolatry of your own image. You are as mute as that gold statue Nebuchadnezzar built. Make all the noise you want—instruments, praise music, blogs full of Christianese. They will be mute unless you humble yourself.

As I shared in Meditation 1 this week, God humbled me not so long ago. He showed me how hardened my heart had become by image management. One of the practical actions of repentance I took was backing off of social media. It feeds my ego, fosters a frenetic mentality, and distracts me from being present with those I love.

But equally as important is the connection I see between social media and the growing anxiety/depression/suicide problem with our youth. While it is a complex conversation and I believe there are many factors that contribute to these dangerous trends, I am convinced after many months of examining data, timelines of the trends, personal behavior, and God's Word that social media and screen use are some of the key factors resulting in unhealthy emotions and living. This makes the example I set on social media a way I either exploit those most at risk or value their life above my personal image goals.

As an influencer, I am convicted to sound an alarm, and to model moderation in the way I use my phone and my social media accounts. I don't believe I can do that while regularly maintaining social media.

Within weeks of repenting and making this and other changes in my life, I noticed a new freshness when I read my Bible. The words seemed more powerful. Messages and meanings were clearer. It was like God put a big ol' megaphone up to my ear and said, "That pleases me."

I'm not saying social media and smartphones are bad. But the way we use them is sometimes not in our best interest or the interest of others. For me, it came down to being addicted to image management.

Maybe you can be on social media and use your smartphone without facing that dilemma. I commend you. As long as God provides peace and you believe it is a valuable use of your time, there's no reason for you to change your habits as I have.

THE GOD WHO SPEAKS

Idols cannot speak. But our God can. He is alive. He does not need a graven image. He does not need a spokesperson. We have a priesthood of believers, so He has every intention of speaking directly to you.

But He will not do it through the superficial noise of our making.

The great revival in the Scottish Hebrides Islands was marked by silence. People who approached the church where the revival began were compelled to stop speaking as they approached. They entered in silence. "The presence of God created fear." Some said it sent shivers down their spines.[17]

Mary Peckham was one young woman who, though resistant to the revival, ultimately surrendered to Christ and spent her life testifying of the miraculous move of His Spirit in the Hebrides. She said:

We don't understand silence. We don't understand reverence. We don't understand! We think that God is in the earthquake. That God is in the wind. That God is in the fire. But as Elijah proved, God was the still, small voice. . . . And we in the Hebrides, we too, as we came into the sanctuary of God, fell silent. And there we were waiting expectantly. . . . All over the congregation—the crowded congregation . . . out would come the handkerchiefs and the sobbing and the sighing silently in the presence of God. That is revival.[18]

Fears of this world scream at you to run. To move. Be busy.
But the fear of God stills you to rest. To stop. Be still.

To the college girl who's afraid she can't make the grade in class and in life, He says, "Be still and know that I am God."

To the woman who's afraid she'll never find the whistle in her work, He says, "Be still and know that I am God."

To the single girl who's afraid of the sound of being alone, He says, "Be still and know that I am God."

To the newlywed who's afraid of the storm of being together, He says, "Be still and know that I am God."

To the overworked single mom who's afraid if she stops she'll never start again, he says, "Be still and know that I am God."

You've made it through another great week of meditation. As we close the week out let God bring to mind any of the things you studied which He might want you to review more carefully. Remember to begin by praying this out loud:

Search me, O God, and know my heart!
Try me and know my thoughts!
And see if there be any grievous way in me,
and lead me in the way everlasting!
(PS. 139:23–24)

For today's prayer activity, I'd like you to get on your knees instead of writing something in this book. The Scripture speaks often of bowing before God. We rarely do it. Sit quietly before Him and be silent. Listen and speak.

Muscle up one last time by completing your weekly meditation assignment.

• *Ask God to identify a Bible verse or sentence that He is prompting you to embrace and understand.*

• *Reword that Bible verse or sentence into a prayer. Ask God what He wants you to do with it. Write a response to Him about what you sense Him saying. Determine in your heart to live it out.*

Amazed! Amazed!

HABAKKUK'S BOOK THROUGH AN END-TIMES LENS

Habakkuk hasn't started to _____ it. Even as he moves into a place of _____, he remains _____ .

The righteous person who lives by faith always has something to _____ about.

God often delivers us _____ our trials not _____ them.

ISAIAH 43:1–4

Live like you're loved.

We will be _____ at how hard the trouble in this world can be.

We will be _____ at how good God can be in the middle of the trouble.

Will you be a woman who passes on a baton of Truth?

Habit #6: Remember to sing praise to God.

Answers to the podcast fill-in-the-blanks can be found on page 216.

WEEK 6

Remember to Sing

In 1851, Sarah Hannah Sheppard gave birth to a baby girl on a Tennessee plantation. Upon hearing that she was to be sold and separated from her husband who was a freedman, she concocted a dark plan. Gathering her daughter in her arms, Sarah headed for the Cumberland River to drown with her daughter.

On her way, she was stopped by Mammy Viney, who cautioned Sarah not to take matters into her own hands, but to trust God. In one report, the old woman raised her eyes to Heaven and said, "Look, Honey, don't you see the clouds of the Lord as they pass by? The Lord has need of this child."[1]

Sarah yielded to the woman's counsel.

Sarah was sold and taken to Mississippi, but not before she was granted permission to sell her daughter, Ella, to her husband for $350.

Ella grew up free, and eventually taught music at Fisk University in Nashville, which was founded in 1866 to educate African Americans after the Civil War. The school was floundering financially, though.

One day the burdened treasurer overheard students singing "plantation songs," which were not meant to be heard in public. He was so moved that he decided to have them arranged for concert performance. Ella rose to the task. The Fisk Jubilee Singers was formed and began to travel widely to raise money for the school. As they did so, they were introducing a new genre of music that had never been heard by most: African American spirituals.

One of the songs she arranged was "Swing Low, Sweet Chariot," which had a dual meaning to slaves who sang it. They yearned for the "chariot" of the Underground Railroad to be used for their freedom, but if not, they would have ultimate freedom in Jesus Christ one day.

Ella eventually found her mother in Mississippi and brought her to Nashville where the two lived together.

Wallace Willis, a former slave from Oklahoma, came forward to claim that he—not Ella—had authored the song,[2] but she unquestionably introduced it to the world.

The true origin of "Swing Low, Sweet Chariot" may remain a mystery along with its biblical root, although some say it's anchored in Ezekiel 1.

Others think it's Habakkuk 3:8, 11.[3]

Either way, that song is just another rendition of one our prophet sang.

MEDITATION 1

Rejoice always

Have you ever had a bummer of a birthday? One everyone forgot or just didn't show up for? Or that arrived right after *the* devastation of your life.

The fires of refinement seem particularly magnified on special days, don't they?

I imagine it could have been like that for the prophet Ezekiel on his thirtieth birthday. Five years earlier, he'd been taken as a captive during the first deportment of the Jews to Babylon. (Daniel, Shadrach, Meshach, and Abednego were not the only faithful followers in exile.)

The way his book sets the stage, he wasn't bellying up to the birthday cake. Rather, he was sitting all alone just outside of the Hebrew refugee camp by the Chebar canal.

Why was he sitting out there by the water all alone?

He was remembering to sing.

That's where they did it. And the Babylonians knew it too (Ps. 137).

One thing is sure: the people of Judah had a habit of singing in captivity.

If they can do it there, can you not rejoice always where you are?

Read Habakkuk 3:1, 19b. Record any observations you have.

Sometimes it's when we feel the least like singing that we need to the most. Habakkuk practiced the habit of remembering to sing praise to God. This week, we're going to dive straight into our list of the six habits.

The Six Habits of Living by Faith

Here is the final habit. Turn to the back of your book, or review the entire list below one last time.

Circle key words that will help you remember the action you need to take for each of them.

1. **Remember to wrestle with God when He seems silent.**
2. **Remember to look to see where God is at work.**
3. **Remember to embed questions for God with Truth.**
4. **Remember to watch for God's answers.**
5. **Remember to fear God.**
6. **Remember to sing praise to God.**

Write the key words or phrases of all six habits on the following lines.

_____

_____

_____

_____

_____

_____

WHEN TO REJOICE

Describe what you know of the prophet's circumstances when he penned this song. (You won't find this answer in the verses we're looking at today, but you've worked hard during this Bible study. You've looked at what happened before Habakkuk wrote this book and what happened after. You know this!)

Habakkuk sings to God in the middle of his devastation. The prophet remembered His faith and chose to trust God no matter his circumstances.

IT'S EASY TO GLORIFY GOD WHEN WE HAVE IT ALL AND EVERYTHING IS GOING WELL, BUT OUR TESTIMONY IS IN THE TEST.

Can we sing His praises when we're in the storms and fires of this life? For it is then that our true character comes out. And what comes out of you is what has been in you. We either truly glorify God for who He is (not what He does or gives), or we find that this test is to purify us of things within us that are not of Him.

WHERE TO REJOICE

Some theologians believe that the Babylonian exile is symbolic of our exile from the garden of Eden. Since we've been banished from that beautiful place due to sin, we await the day when we can live in our perfect home: heaven. The ache we feel when life is not good is to remind us of where we truly belong. When a common thread pops up, I chase it down to see if it's possibly a mini-symbol to learn from.

Look ahead to tomorrow's meditation. Skim Habakkuk 3:2–15. Circle any reference to water or bodies of water. How many do you find?

Read Ezekiel 1:1. Where is this prophet of God when he receives his vision from God?

TIME FOR TIMELINES!
Turn to pages 222–223 in the back of the book.

Find 593 BC on the timeline. Write in: "Ezekiel begins to prophesy on July 31." [4]

It's been five years since Ezekiel was carried off to Babylon with the first group of exiles. It's his thirtieth birthday—and the day he would have been installed as a priest, he's sitting on the bank of an irrigation canal.

Read Psalm 137:1–4. What does it reveal about this same body of water?

In the Old Testament, water usually symbolized God's blessings being freely poured out for His people. When the exiles mentioned water or sat by it to sing, they were reminding God that He held a holy pitcher of overflowing favor in His hand. They were also reminding themselves that one day He would pour it out.

Read John 7:37–39. Where should we position ourselves to sing as New Testament believers?

There's no faster way to lose your song than to stop sitting with other Holy Spirit-filled believers. Each is filled with a stream of Living Water. Together they're a powerful force—a life-giving river.

Some of my most thirst-quenching moments with the body of Christ do not happen on Sunday morning but in more relaxed environments where we can take each other's spiritual pulses and provide life-giving CPR where needed. I realize the church is not perfect. (I think that's why we needed a Savior to begin with.) But you cannot have spiritual life without being attached to the full body.

If it's been a while, get your beloved self into a community of believers who can remind your heart to sing.

WHY WE REJOICE

Look at Habakkuk 3:19b. Who does Habakkuk hand this song to when he's finished writing it and with what instructions? What can you assume he expects and why?

As I sit here, I'm waiting for my teakettle to whistle signaling that the water is ready to be used. It reminds me of the reason I sing.

When I was twenty-six, ministry was birthed out of a testimony of God's forgiveness of my sexual sin. When God healed my broken heart and removed the cloak of shame, the comfort boiled up inside of me. I was like a teakettle with steam pressurizing inside. There was not a single thing I could do but make some noise and let others know my story. It was hard for me to describe to others what was happening, but then I found a Bible verse that helped me.

Read 2 Corinthians 1:3–4. Why does God comfort you when you go through devastating times? What do you need to do in response?

Like Habakkuk, I wrote my story down. My book *And the Bride Wore White: Seven Secrets to Purity* continues to encourage broken hearts almost twenty-five years later.

You may never be an author or songwriter, but your testimony of God's faithfulness needs to be shared with others. Write it down, speak it out, sing a song but whatever you do, pass it on. It will be a lifeline of hope to someone still mired in the questions and doubts.

Excuse me, I've got to go.

I hear a teakettle singing.

Each day of our final week together, I'd like you to begin your prayer time by practicing the habit of singing. You may feel prompted by the Lord to use a song that's meaningful to you, but I'll also suggest one for you each day.

The song I've selected today reflects, I think, the swift pace and mood changes of what is called a Shigionoth in the Psalms. This way you can imagine the tenor of Habakkuk's song. It's also a great example of how someone—whether Ella or Wallace—wrote a testimony of hope while a captive in our own nation simply because of the color of their skin. God forgive us!

Listen to "Swing Low, Sweet Chariot" by Etta James.[5]

Write a prayer to God. Today I'd like you to remember a time He rescued or sustained you. Put your testimony of God's faithfulness on paper as a prayer of thanksgiving. It needs to be shared with others, and sometimes writing it down is great practice for when we need to pull it up and pass it on with our mouths.

MEDITATION 2

Remember to sing when you don't feel like it

We're going to study a big chunk of poetry today.

May it spark your imagination!

Sometimes our imagination is a scalpel. The one we take to memories gone so bad that they've become wounds that won't heal . . . because somewhere along the way we forgot. Your imagination lets you look back to remember your understanding of how God was at work during painful times. It helps you get your history right.

The object of your greatest pain can become the source of your greatest blessing when you offer it to God.

—CORRIE TEN BOOM,[6] HOLOCAUST SURVIVOR

Today, I'm going to ask you to be brave.

Will you let God help you see what He was working to do during the deepest pain in your past?

Read Habakkuk 3:2–15. Record any observations you have.

Circle the word fear. *How is this word evidence of Habakkuk's faith?*

What does the prophet petition God to do in verse 2? Why?

Wait! I thought all this time it was Habakkuk who had amnesia. Is it God who actually has a memory problem, or is the poetry hinting at something else?

REMINDING GOD TO REMEMBER

Read Isaiah 49:15. What does this say about God's memory?

A mother's love is considered the strongest this world can offer. God says that His affection supersedes even that. The heart of a mother is God's true nature. He will not forget us. So, Habakkuk has to be hinting at something else.

What could Habakkuk be referring to? (You may already know, but Genesis 9:1 and Luke 1:54, 72 could be helpful to you if you need them.)

Time to muscle up on our understanding of *covenant*. This promissory agreement was a blend of law (that bound them to the terms of their contract) and love (that served as a safeguard should one of them fail to meet the terms). Our modern marriage license is a good comparison, but a pale shadow of covenant law and love, but the two parties were considered family bonded by faithfulness at any cost.

"I will be yours. You will be mine."

The covenant placed the riches and influence of each party at the beck and call of the other. If partner A ran out of grain, partner B's grain would be at-the-ready.

"What's mine is yours. What's yours is mine."

The kind of love expressed in covenant was a class all its own. Because the relationship intended faithfulness at any cost, the love was mingled with mercy.

Draw a rainbow above the word mercy *in Habakkuk 3:2.*

After a covenant was established, faithful partners called upon it. When they did so, it was called—wait for it—remembering! Habakkuk is referencing the unconditional love that marks a covenant in this verse.

Draw a rainbow above the word remember *in Habakkuk 3:2.*

God remembers His covenant with the Jewish people. And if you have surrendered your life to Jesus Christ, you are a partner in the New Covenant. He remembers you.

We're the ones that keep forgetting. God knew we would. That's why He put Abram to sleep when He walked through the bloody pieces. Habakkuk is living in the messy middle of Judah's inability to keep its side of the deal.

Enter Jesus. But, the Jews—imagine this—have some questions and doubts!

The book of Hebrews is written to Jewish believers to answer some of the questions they have that could tempt them to abandon their faith. Reading it since I began my study of Habakkuk has been a bit mind-blowing. I understand it like never before. I'd like you to read a bit of it right now. I have no questions for you to consider. I simply ask that you lean into these words as if they are what they are: the very words of God. May His Spirit rest heavily on you as you read them.

Read Hebrews 6:13–20; 7:22; 8:1–13; 10:15–17, 35–39. Jot down anything God's Spirit speaks to you.

Habakkuk understands the unfailing love of covenant, too. In 3–15, he traces the history of the world to invoke "remembrance" of God's covenant with His people.

Comb through Habakkuk 3:4–15 and bracket off sections as you recognize the historical events the prophet was referencing. The two big ones are Creation and the Exodus. Make a list below of all the ways God has shown His might, love, or faithfulness according to these verses.

Let's focus in on the Exodus for just a moment. It was certainly one of many peaks in a long history of Jewish persecution. Imagine with me that you are Miriam, the sister of Moses. You've just crossed the Red Sea. That in itself was no small task. Today this 1,300-mile long inlet of the Indian Ocean is two hundred miles wide in many places. And has an average depth of just over 1,000 feet. Talk about your tired dogs! My feet would be screaming.

But you didn't just walk across it. (Though future records will indicate that you were smart enough to find a narrow spot to cross!) You went in haste with an angry horde hunting your people down. At the last moment, the miraculous curtain of water God had pulled back falls. And Pharaoh is destroyed with his army. You're standing there dumbfounded.

Based on your common reactions to life's challenges, what are you most likely to say? Check one.

___ *(Read with anger.) I can't take any more of this! We could have been swallowed by that water ourselves. I'm out!*

___ *(Read with sarcasm.) Well, that's just great. What are we gonna do if our plan doesn't work out? We can't go back now!*

___ *(Read with genuine joy.) This seems like a good time to get all the girls together for a sing-along!*

Is the glass half empty or is it half full? If you look at life through the lens of God's covenant promise and His historical faithfulness, it will always be half full. And He's got His holy pitcher of Living Water ready to refresh you when He sees you truly need it.

Miriam knew this, and that gave her freedom from worldly fear and anxiety. She spoke like a woman who feared God. That meant she was poised to bow before, to worship, to submit to, and to stand in awe of Him.

Which is exactly what she did on the other side of the Red Sea.

Read Exodus 15:20. Record who sang with Miriam and what instruments they used to worship God.

Read Exodus 12:31–36. Why might it be odd that these women all had their tambourines?

Forced to vacate her home in the darkness, Miriam would have had little time to pack. Pharaoh had changed his mind before. They had to get out while the getting was good.

Imagine Miriam frantically packing.

Let's see. Food . . . emmer wheat, barley, and oil. I'll grab the herbs on the way out. Gee! That bread has not risen, and it's not baked, but it'll have to do. Medicine . . . honey, abra-ointment, setseft-seeds. Got 'em. Uhmmm . . . Some animal skins for the cool nights. Oh, wait! I almost forgot something important! Just need to grab . . . my tambourine.

A tambourine?

I don't think all those women ended up with tambourines by the Red Sea unless they had a solid conviction that worship was warfare!

And their language would have reminded them. The same word that was used to describe a blow in battle (Judges 4:21)—taqa[7]—was also used to describe clapping their hands in worship (Ps. 47:1, 2). I believe those tambourines were well worn before they arrived at the Red Sea. And I imagine Pharaoh may have heard them not knowing they were a declaration of the mighty clap of God that the Red Sea would bring to his reign.

A woman who knows her God packs her tambourine to praise Him on the dark nights and the brightest of days.

Have you been using yours?

The song I've selected today invites us to meditate on our ultimate hope, as there is . . .

. . . salvation in no one else [but Jesus], for there is no other name under heaven given among men by which we must be saved.
(ACTS 4:12)

Read that verse out loud before you listen to the next song, and notice the covenant language embedded within it. When a lesser covenant partner invoked the authority of a greater covenant partner to a third party, they used their name. They would say, "I am here in the name of _____."

Do you see it? The beauty of praying in Jesus' name? Of stating that you are being and shall be ultimately in the covenant love authority of Jesus Christ? When you bow to the name of Jesus, you are invoking His ultimate promise. This means ultimate rescue.

Now, it's time to write a prayer to God. Today I'd like you to remember a painful time in your past that seems unresolved. Perhaps it is even still painful. Sing this song specifically over that memory.

PAUSE TO REFLECT

Listen to "The Lord is My Salvation" by Shane & Shane.[8]

Now, sit quietly and ask God to give you eyes to see how He has been at work all along to be your salvation even there in that difficult time. Write a prayer of gratitude to Him.

Remember to sing when you're terrified

FAST FORWARD TO BABYLON >>>

I'm pretty sure ten-year-old Willie Myrick was terrified when he was kidnapped from his Atlanta home. He was playing with his pet Chihuahua in the front yard when a stranger drove up, lured him into the car, and drove off.

The kidnapper said he did not want to hear a word from the boy. But Willie began to sing.

He sang a popular gospel song, offering praise to the Lord. His kidnapper was angered and yelled at him to be quiet.

But the boy continued singing. For three hours.[9]

Finally, the criminal grew tired of Willie's joyful song and kicked him out of the car.

The boy told reporters: "If you praise the Lord, He will help you in mysterious ways."[10]

Do you believe that? I mean, do you really live your life in such a way that your times of terror turn to tunes of trust?

Read Habakkuk 3:16–18. Record any observations you have.

Habakkuk may have rustled up his worship, but he's still speaking transparently. Circle all the references to the condition of his body at the news of his circumstances. Write the list below.

Our modern translations cloak the vulnerability of Habakkuk's lyrics a bit more than I prefer. A more direct translation of "my body trembles" would be "my bowels trembled."[11] (Can you say tummy problems?)

What do these physical symptoms reveal about his emotional condition?

Have you ever faced a problem so troubling that your body manifested telltale signs of it? Write about it below. List all the physical signs you experienced.

Emotional wellness is not the absence of negative emotions. Neither is it giving in to them. I don't know about you, but I'm prone to the drastic extremes of denying my true feelings or letting them be the boss of me. Unless I make a deliberate choice to respond based on the Truth I know in my head, my heart gets overwhelmed.

Habakkuk models a better way.

"YET I WILL REJOICE"

Read Habakkuk 3:17–18. Circle all the different references to produce and livestock.

What do you think these would represent to Habakkuk back in the day?

That might sound like a bad day on a hobby farm to you and to me, but to Habakkuk it was his national and personal economic portfolio. With no livestock or harvest, he would soon be destitute. As would all the friends and the family he loved.

On top of that, he was likely wrestling with images of bloodshed at the hands of the Babylonians and wondering who he would lose.

With that scene in his imagination, what does he intend to do?

Read Philippians 4:4–9. Let's ruminate on a familiar Truth.

Why do you think the apostle Paul repeats himself in the first verse?

When we feel anxious, what are we told to do?

What will the result be? Describe it thoroughly.

Tomorrow, we will look closely at Habakkuk 3:19 but I want you to consider one thing about that verse today. The last phrase reads "To the choirmaster: with stringed instruments." Based on that, what can you assume about Habakkuk 3:16-18? Why would Habakkuk hand this poetry to his community's worship leader?

We often believe the lie that joy and peace cannot coexist with fear and grief. In fact, they are concurrent with one another. Our anxiety and sorrow become joy and peace when we use them to drive our thoughts to God. Acknowledge the emotions, but don't give them the last word. That belongs to Jesus. You get to choose.

Almost two decades ago, Bob and I made an intentional decision to look at our times of stress as an opportunity to discover the joy and peace of Jesus Christ. We wrote our own definition of *joy* and asked a friend to write it on the walls of our family room with a permanent black Sharpie. (She had really pretty handwriting!)

JOY (re-member)	*noun.* The confident conviction that God is in control of everything.

How does this definition comfort or challenge you?

Singing is one way we can meditate on God's Truth when we are afraid. But does it work?

Let's be mindful of the fact that the verses we're studying today are lyrics. Since Habakkuk 3:19 hands these words over to the worship leader, we can imagine that faithful Jews would have sung them in the temple at Jerusalem as the Babylonian terror approached. Songs are not easily forgotten. They stick in our minds forever. Therefore, I'd like to believe the words Habakkuk wrote were one of the songs the Hebrews lifted when they gathered by the Chebar canal during exile. If the words have efficacy, they should have helped a good Hebrew or two through some hard years.

Buckle up for one last fast-forward trip into Babylon. We'll land our time machine just about the time the entire nation is bowing down to King Nebuchadnezzar's big gold statue.

Read Daniel 3:8–30. What's similar about this story and what Habakkuk writes in 3:17–18?

Habakkuk faces a test to see if he will bow to fear and doubt. Shadrach, Meshach, and Abednego face a test to see if they will bow to idols. Circle anything below that you've been tempted to bow to in recent years. What wants to be your god?

anxiety	romance	unbelief
self-pity	sex	popularity
materialism	unforgiveness/bitterness	power
perfection	family expectations	workaholism
food	drugs	alcohol
hopelessness	purposelessness	depression

Both Habakkuk and the other men pass their tests with flying colors. Their circumstances do not determine their state of mind nor what they will bow to.

Habakkuk contrasts his circumstances and ultimate response with three words. So do the three men in the fiery furnace. In essence, they are using language to draw a proverbial line in the sand. Find the lines and fill in the blanks.

HABAKKUK	_____ _____ _____
SHADRACH, MESHACH, & ABEDNEGO	_____ _____ _____

I do believe Habakkuk would have been honored if he heard about these three men. There's a strong parallel between the song Habakkuk wrote and the one they live in that fiery furnace.

What does Daniel 3:24-25 tell us did *burn up in the fire? What might that mean symbolically for us when we face our trials?*

If we stand on God's Truth, not only will we experience joy and peace that's beyond comprehension this side of the flames, but we will also be set free. The fire loses its power to burn us, but it licks through our bondage and becomes our freedom. The fire becomes our freedom when it burns the unbelief right out of us.

But that only happens if you draw a line in the sand and choose to respond with rejoicing. Today I'm going to give you a chance to let the flames burn some bonds off your life.

Let's get to our prayer work!

Today's song is a bit like the one Habakkuk wrote and which I believe Shadrack, Meshach, and Abednego sang! Horatio Spafford wrote the lyrics in 1873 after a season of devastation on top of devastation. His two-year-old son was killed in the Great Chicago Fire in 1871. His successful business fell apart as a result of the economic downturn the city faced. Then, his four daughters drowned when a ship crossing the Atlantic Ocean sank. Shortly thereafter, he travelled by boat to meet his grieving wife. When the vessel passed near where his daughters died, he penned the words to "It Is Well."

One hundred and twenty-five years later, we're still medicating our souls when we meditate through this song. Essentially, we're saying, "yet I will rejoice."

PAUSE TO REFLECT

Listen to "It Is Well" by Caleb & Kelsey.[12]

Write your own "Yet I will rejoice" song today. List some things that aren't going well in life right now or that you're concerned are heading in a bad direction for your life. End your song with a commitment to rejoice in the Lord no matter what.

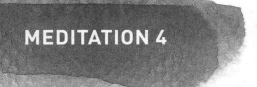

MEDITATION 4

Remember to sing what you believe

I put this Bible study to paper during a hard season.

During the writing of this meditation, I read through my prayer journal from the previous year. Somehow what I read took me off guard. It was as if I was not the woman who'd written those entries recounting days of sheer insanity.

And there sure were an extra lot of them.

I'm as transparent as they come and have a written core value that reminds me that we overcome the enemy by "the blood of the Lamb" and "the word of our testimony" (Rev. 12:11). Whatever parts of my story God can use to bring others closer to Him, I surrender in radical vulnerability.

But some of that year may always remain sealed up for my heart alone. There were days so ugly, only Jesus and my best friend should ever see how I showed up.

On top of those secret battles was a public one to keep my head above water.

You remember that high-risk pregnancy that had me praying with our son, Robby and dear daughter-in-law, Aleigha? The kinds of prayers that begged God to show up?

He did.

And with clouds.

The evening Addie and Zoe arrived safely into this world, the sunset turned the sky—and a single pair of cloud streaks—pink. Like a promise.

Caring for preemies is not for the faint of heart, but two of them? It takes a small army of the sleepless. For eleven weeks, our home was full of joy as the new family of four blessed us as house guests and the front door was revolving as anyone willing to hold a baby or change a diaper came and went.

Did I mention we were also planning the wedding of our Autumn to Jacob? And that we were nervously waiting for his VISA approval so he could come here from Taiwan?

And that our beloved Lexi, who'd managed her money diligently for many years, bought her first home? And had left a position at an international branding agency in Detroit to temporarily help my ministry to tween girls re-brand?

Burping bibs. And catering menus. A real estate deal. And a feeding schedule. One massive marketing plan. And an infant CPR lesson. The big Welcome-to-the-World-Addie-and-Zoe party. And an elegant garden bridal shower. Blessings, all of them.

But I was worn out from all the raindrops.

(And . . . cue the bulging disc scene!)

No wonder my dear daughter Autumn once dubbed it our "summer of joyful chaos."

My journal became a declaration of what I could not yet see but had faith to believe.

The summer had not even started—

no healthy babies . . . yet,

no VISA for my daughter's fiancé . . . yet,

and no house to be found . . . yet—

but I began to declare it would submit to the promises of God. I wrote:

> *May 5 – "All my children shall be taught by the LORD, and great shall be the peace of your children." Isaiah 54:13 . . . I will look back on you, Summer of 2019, and this verse will be true. In righteousness they will be established.*

Sometimes you just have to pray what you believe!

Or sing it.

Most of my journal is full of the lyrics of the songs I was singing during that time. The first entry is a sketch of a sword and this resolution from the song by Christy Nockels based on the description of the armor of God referenced in the book of Ephesians:

"His Word will be the sword you keep."[13]

My dear friend Jennifer had given me an album called *Be Held: Lullabies for the Beloved.* It's laden with scriptural truth, and it's not really for babies. It's for grown women who are in a fierce daily battle to remember.

One of the songs is titled "Always Remember to Never Forget!"

I don't know what challenges you have faced while we've been getting to know each other and our good friend Habakkuk, but I know this: sometimes you have to sing what you believe so you remember not to forget.

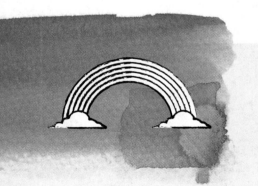

You've made it to the very end of our prophet's poem. Read Habakkuk 3:19. Record your observations on the closing verse of his song.

Circle the word my *each time it appears in this verse. Write the three nouns or objects that follow the pronoun below, and let's begin to sort out what all these possessive pronouns mean.*

MY STRENGTH

Put a rainbow above the words "God," "the Lord," and "my." What is Habakkuk invoking one last time as he completes his song?

Compare Habakkuk 1:2 with today's verse. What's changed?

The wrestler is now in full embrace. Habakkuk has progressed from full out wrestling in chapter one to a gentler grip in chapter two and a warm, possessive embrace in chapter three.

We don't know how much time there was between the writing of these chapters, but there's a marked difference in the relationship. God is not a distant deity with whom the prophet is frustrated, but an intimate partner who makes Habakkuk feel safe. And loved. Where earlier the references to covenant are less intimate, this one is marked by passion.

Do you have passion for Jesus? A personal relationship with Him is essential to weathering difficult times. Are you experiencing that kind of intimacy with God? It's ok if you are not. You made it this far into the study and so I assume you're wrestling it out. I commend you for that, and you're headed in the right direction. Give yourself grace as you grow in your understanding of Him.

MY HIGH PLACES

Take an educated guess at what "my high places" is referring to.

The "high places" or "heights" in Habakkuk 3:19 are not speaking of just any mountain or hill, but those that surround Jerusalem (Ps. 125:2). Three prominent hills surround the city— Mount Moriah, the Mount of Olives, and Mount Zion. (Sound familiar?) Each connects to several deep, rocky valleys. This made the location a natural fortress hiding it from enemies. Approaching the holy city was so challenging that foreign invaders traveling through often simply went around it.

Read Genesis 17:7. When God made a covenant with Abram to give him the land of Jerusalem, how long did He promise the deed would last?

When Habakkuk declares that God makes him able to walk on "my" high places, he is singing what he believes—that though the hills of Jerusalem will be taken from God's people, one day they'll be the possession of the Hebrew people forever.

I do so wish you were here with me right now. I'd invite you to pull on your cowgirl boots and mosey on out to the Gresh barn with me. There I would introduce you to two of the most loved goats on the planet: Cindy Lou Who and Boo Who. (All my goats are named after Dr. Seuss characters. Yes, I realize Boo Who is a loose application of the theme. Talk to Farmer Bob about it.)

When my Cindy and Boo were just weeks old, I took them for a walk to help them discover their secret super power—climbing. There was a huge tree down in my woods and if they would jump on the trunk it would bring them to eye level with me.

When we arrived, I did not have to lift them or suggest they climb. They looked at the obstacle in the path and quickly deduced that it was a giant playground just for them. When they discovered their super power, they began leaping off the log and climbing right back up to it.

The deer Habakkuk is writing about is probably one he's seen before—perhaps in the Lebanon forest. The best guess is that they were Persian fallow deer, which look kind of like American white-tailed deer, but they never lose their spots. They have the same types of hooves as my goaties, giving them the ability to walk in difficult places.

Habakkuk realizes that his feet have changed since he first wrote Habakkuk 1:1. The tough times have pushed him to the heights where the enemy has less access to him.

Read Song of Songs 2:8. What imagery does this passage offer of Christ coming toward you (or me) for intimacy?

Up here . . . on the mountains . . . you can find intimacy with God.

I found that in a new way while I was writing this Bible study. I have to say, this was not an easy project. It pushed me and stretched me, and I seemed unable to write about well-learned life lessons before the Lord took me through a fresh lesson to relearn it. It pushed me to the heights.

One Sunday, I found myself gloriously all alone at home. I was sitting quietly and listening to the Lord. But I was distracted. So, I decided to play a worship song and doodle.

Lately, I'd been practicing my listening by asking the Lord what song He would have me sing to Him. Often a song I have not heard for some time pops into my mind. And when I play it, there's a special sense of true worship in my heart.

On that day, I felt like God wanted me to play an "old" song. That's all I knew.

What could be old? Hmmm . . . Oh, Rich Mullins. Very old.

I love the meaningful lyrics this man left behind for us when he went home to be with the Lord. Rich fought his faith out hard as he battled addiction. Toward the end of his life, he found peace by separating himself from the loud world and living on a quiet Indian reservation in the West. Though his songs were lucrative, he only received a modest salary. Though I do not agree with all of Rich's theology, I am inspired by many of his authentic choices.

I played through many of my Rich Mullins songs that day, but none of them felt like the one. It seemed I had not heard the Lord correctly.

I was discouraged.

Still, I started my search again, but this time looked online instead of on my music app. Within moments, I stumbled across one I had never heard before. It was on YouTube. I pushed play. The sound of a very old, very poor recording of Rich in concert began to fill my living room.

And tears fell because I knew it was the "old" song.

I listened to that one all afternoon. For four and a half hours I felt the nearness of my Lord and worshipped Him with such intimacy that at times I was surprised by it.

I think we leapt a bit on the hills that day.

How very much He loves me.

May you discover that He loves you just as intimately.

MAY GOD GIVE YOU FEET FOR YOUR PATH,

NOT A PATH FOR YOUR FEET.

You can probably guess which song I'd like you to hear today.

PAUSE TO REFLECT

Listen to "The Joy of Jesus" by Rich Mullins (featuring Matt Maher, Mac Powell, Ellie Holcomb.)[14]

May the joy of Jesus be with you, my friend. And may you dance and laugh and sing. May you know the warmth of His embrace. Sit in it quietly today and know that He loves you.

Remember to sing like you're loved

Since I started writing this study for you, I've learned that many believe the book of Habakkuk is primarily a theodicy. Don't know what that is? I had to look it up.

THEODICY
(the-a-de-se)

noun. A defense of God's goodness and omnipotence in view of the existence of evil.[15]

As you're about to close the pages of this book, I hope you've found the word of God to be very alive and active and capable of defending the goodness and omnipotence of God no matter the evil you may be facing. I have prayed that God would use this study to answer your questions and doubts and to revive your faith.

Have you also seen how God humbles prideful people even as He lets the righteous who live by faith experience great joy?

God may seem silent at times, but He always has a plan to deal with the evil . . . eventually. Habakkuk encourages me. I can wait on the Lord—and so can you—in confidence that He will work out everything for our good (Rom. 8:28).

Let's talk about the word *eventually*.

We've not yet begun our study time for today, but it seems appropriate to tackle one last plotting on our timeline right here.

TIME FOR TIMELINES!

Turn to pages 222–223 in the back of the book.

Find 538 BC on the timeline. Write: "Exiles return home."[16]

In 538, King Cyrus of Babylon decreed that the exiles could return to their homeland of Judah.

God may not fix your world tomorrow. Things could, as they did for Habakkuk, get much worse before they get better. But God does *eventually* work things for our good.

I want to point something out about our *eventually* today. Habakkuk—who by now is a dear friend to us—was a prophet. I imagine that as he recorded his conversation with God about good and evil, he could not help but let a little foretelling of future events leak out of him. This was very significant to me as I studied Habakkuk. It bolstered my confidence in the Scriptures.

How did a man who lived between 612–588 BC know about events that would not happen until the future?

Everything revealed to Habakkuk was fulfilled.

- The Chaldeans, an itty-bitty people group, were raised up to power. (Hab. 1:6)
- Through the Babylonian empire they became a mighty empire. (1:7–11)
- They carried the Hebrews off as captives. (1:14–17)
- But God eventually brought mighty Babylon to its knees. (2:4–20)
- And His people were delivered back to their promised land. (3:8–15)

Habakkuk may have used his watchtower to get a good view of God's big plan for the nations, but you and I are in an even better position to "look" and "see." Our past perspective fills the tank of our faith engine with far more fuel than he could have imagined.

And we have much more to look back upon.

- Our Messiah came from the line of David. Judah was right to protect the lineage. (Isa. 11:1)
- He was born in Bethlehem "among the clans of Judah" even though that seemed impossible to those who lived through the Babylonian exile. (Micah 5:2)
- He endured the ultimate "oppression and judgment" and was "taken away" to fulfill the old covenant and bring one that Hebrews 8:6 would declare to be "established on better promises." (Isa. 53:1–8)

And now we are here.

Holding this baton of faith.

Waiting for the rest of God's story of redemption to unfold.

Eventually.

Welcome to your final meditation. Our look at Habakkuk is largely complete but begs a final thought. We'll dive into Isaiah 42:1–10 today for our last study time together.

Read Isaiah 42:1–10. Then, answer these questions.

Who do you think Isaiah is referring to when he uses the words "my servant"?

What is the promise of "my servant"?

Write down any promises of "my servant" that you need to hold onto right now.

Isaiah refers to Israel as "servant" elsewhere (Isa. 49:3). But the nation walks in that ideal one day only through the Messiah, Jesus Christ (Matt. 2:15; Hosea 11:1).[17] Jesus is the deliverer of these promises. And I believe He will fulfill them. Even more so having watched the prophecy of Habakkuk unfold.

Read Isaiah 42:8, 9 in the version below and underline anything that fills you with a ripple of hope.

"I am the Lord; that is my name!
   I will not give my glory to anyone else,
   nor share my praise with carved idols.

Everything I prophesied has come true,
   and now I will prophesy again.
I will tell you the future before it happens."
(ISA. 42:8, 9 NLT)

I heard this version of those verses read on a podcast recently, and it planted so much hope in me for the troubles of my world. God's Word does not fail. He still enables the righteous who live by faith to experience great joy. You and I may desire for God to change the parts of our world that are broken, but that does not have to happen in order for us to experience peace, hope, and joy. We have an ultimate hope in Christ's return. And that makes something erupt within us.

Look at Isaiah 42:10. What did this prophet also do as a result of his awareness of God's sovereignty and goodness?

Both Habakkuk and Isaiah find themselves compelled to sing. And they invite us to do the same, no matter what's going on in our lives. No matter how dark things get in this world. It's a beautiful part of practicing this sometimes difficult task of living by faith and knowing that God is good even if He does not fix things in our lifetime.

As I finish up the first draft of this book, China has quarantined forty million residents as experts predict that, if not contained, the coronavirus pandemic could kill sixty-five million people.[18] (On the last day of editing, what had become COVID-19 had infected a confirmed 1.4 million and the death toll had just passed 81,000.[19])

NASA is hosting an animated video of how a devastating season of unprecedented Australian wildfires could impact the globe with hurricanes.[20]

A rocket has reportedly hit the US Embassy compound in Iraq, which is the site of Babylon so many years ago.[21]

But Habakkuk has girded me with the certainty that I'm going to be OK.

Maybe you sense that hope too.

This brings me back to Habakkuk 1:5—the verse where God told our dear friend of a prophet that he would be doubly amazed if he knew what God was up to! Here's where it gets really good. (Can you say "twist?")

AMAGED! AMAZED!

I do think we often take Habakkuk 1:5 out of context.

And I don't.

Because it is true that the verse comes just before God tells Habakkuk that He's going to use a wicked world force to discipline His children. But it is also true that Habakkuk clearly finds amazing intimacy and peace in spite of those circumstances. What terrified him at one point, no longer does. He is comforted by the intimacy He has discovered while he embraces our covenant God.

That is what I find most amazing about Habakkuk's faith.

Even if our world is falling apart, we can trust the covenant promises of God and experience authentic joy.

I think God was telling Habakkuk that it was going to be worse than he could imagine; but the joy he would learn to experience in the middle of it was going to be better than he could imagine. God was saying:

You won't believe how bad the world can be!
And you won't believe how good I can be!

I must note that we do not know if Habakkuk went into exile with the rest of the Judean people or if he witnessed God's deliverance of the exiles back to Jerusalem. We just know that his writings end in prayerful praise (Hab. 3).

We do know that Daniel did not get to return with his beloved citizens of Judah. We don't know why. Perhaps it was because he'd aged seventy years by then and the long trek home would have been too much for his body. Another possibility is that he'd become such a significant influence on the pagan kings of Babylon and could have felt that in staying he was fulfilling work as a missionary of sorts. I imagine that Daniel's heart most certainly longed for home from time to time, but his *eventually* never reunited his feet with the sod he grew up on. His writings end in prayer, too (Dan. 9).

Let us be people of prayer and praise no matter what our circumstances because eventually, we're going to see the King of kings set all things right. For now, I'll do my best to live by faith and rejoice in whatever circumstances the Lord assigns to me.

It's my prayer that you will too. And that you'll never look at this little three-chapter book the same again. And that no matter your trials or the violence of a sinful world, you will never forget to remember God's faithfulness and live in the unbelievable joy it produces.

PAUSE TO REFLECT ONE LAST TIME

Select a song that brings you joy. No, wait! Listen for God's Spirit to prompt you toward a song that will wrap your heart in the joy of His goodness and sovereignty.

ACKNOWLEDGMENTS

For as long as I can remember, my mother—Kay Barker—prayed these words over my life.

"Look, and be amazed! You will be astounded at what I am about to do! For I am going to do something in your own lifetime that you will have to see to believe." (HAB. 1:5 TLB)

I have no doubt that God knew one day that I'd write this study, but I certainly had no ambition of my own to pursue this project. In recent years, my friends at Moody Publishers had been asking if I'd write a Bible study. At the time, I was finishing up some coursework with my denomination, the Christian & Missionary Alliance, that required me to thoroughly study a book of the Bible.

Why not publish it? I thought.

When I approached my pastor and coach, Jonathan Weibel, I made a solid case for a book of the Bible that I thought would make a great study. He looked unimpressed and asked if I had considered anything else. For some reason, the word Habakkuk popped out of my mouth. Something stirred in him, and he convinced me to write this.

I'm so grateful.

Early encouragement came from a few who did the homework of the first few lessons to see if it even worked. Thank you to my cheerleading squad: Lexi Gresh, Eileen King, Aubrey Brush, Sonya Ley, Ellie Siebel, and Michaela Jones.

I'm grateful for Professors Chris Miller (Cedarville University) and Bryan Litfin (Moody Bible Institute) for both consulting and advising as I navigated unfamiliar theological territory. They were such gentle mentors.

Then, my faithful long-time partnership with Moody Publishers kicked into high gear as we worked from our homes during the COVID-19 quarantine to edit, design, and market what had suddenly become a very relevant tool for the body of Christ to learn how to talk to God during difficult times. Judy Dunagan, Amanda Cleary Eastep, Erik Peterson, Ashley Torres, Randall Payleitner, and Paul Santhouse have been my co-laborers for Christ.

And, my beloved Bob Gresh sacrifices greatly with every project I write and is my most trusted advisor as each comes to life.

But mostly, thank you to the One True, Omnipotent God who is always in control and is unfolding a good plan, even when it seems evil is unleashed in our lives.

"Remember this and stand firm,
    recall it to mind . . .
    remember the former things of old;
for I am God, and there is no other;
    I am God, and there is none like me . . .
And I will accomplish all my purpose . . .
I have spoken, and I will bring it to pass;
    I have purposed, and I will do it."
(ISA. 46:8–11)

NOTES

Week 1

1. Michael Rydelnik, "Habakkuk," in *The Moody Bible Commentary*, ed. Michael Rydelnik and Michael Vanlaningham (Chicago: Moody Publishers, 2014), 1387.
2. John 8:22–25.
3. "Remember," Dictionary.com, https://www.dictionary.com/browse/remember?s=t.
4. Timothy J. Keller, "Rejoicing in Tribulation," Sermon, Gospel in Life, New York City, June 7, 2009.
5. Ibid.
6. Max Lucado, *Unshakable Hope: Building Our Lives on the Promises of God* (Nashville: Thomas Nelson, 2018), 4.
7. "Faith," Dictionary.com, https://www.dictionary.com/browse/faith?s=t.
8. Henry T. Blackaby and Claude V. King, *Experiencing God: Knowing and Doing the Will of God* (Youth Edition) (Nashville: Lifeway, 1994), 11.
9. Caleb Parke, "Bible App announces 'most popular Bible verse' of 2019," Fox News, December 6, 2019, https://www.foxnews.com/faith-values/bible-verse-popular-app-2019.
10. James Swanson, *Dictionary of Biblical Languages with Semantic Domains: Hebrew (Old Testament)* 1997: n.p., print (retrieved on Logos).
11. *New Living Translation Illustrated Study Bible* (Carol Stream, IL: Tyndale, 2015), 649.
12. Ibid., 1594.
13. "Covenant," Merriam-Webster.com, https://www.merriam-webster.com/dictionary/covenant.
14. Robin Ngo, "At Carthage, Child Sacrifice?" *Biblical Archeology*, April 1, 2018, https://www.biblicalarchaeology.org/daily/ancient-cultures/daily-life-and-practice/at-carthage-child-sacrifice.
15. *New Living Translation Illustrated Study Bible* (Carol Stream, IL: Tyndale, 2015), 1594.
16. Ibid.
17. Andrew Knowles, *The Bible Guide*, 1st ed. (Minneapolis,: Augsburg, 2001), print (retrieved on Logos).

Week 2

1. "Amy Carmichael Helped the Helpless," *Christianity* (blog), July 16, 2010, https://www.christianity.com/church/church-history/church-history-for-kids/amy-carmichael-helped-the-helpless-11634859.html.
2. I struggled with whether to write this paragraph in present or past tense. The devadasi still exists today in India. Women still suffer under the misogynistic, pagan view that they are a "god servant." They often feel that they must dedicate one of their daughters to the same life, or risk the anger of the god or goddess to whom they are aligned. Men use them in the name of religion. By the age of forty or so, their bodies are ravaged by sexually transmitted disease including HIV/AIDs. Indrani Nayar-Gall, "How 10,000 devadasis live their lives in Karnataka," April 9, 2018, *Times of India*, https://timesofindia.indiatimes.com/city/bengaluru/sexual-servitude-to-the-gods/articleshow/63660465.cms.
3. Pamela Rose Williams, "21 Top Amy Carmichael Quotes," https://www.whatchristianswanttoknow.com/21-top-amy-carmichael-quotes.
4. Richard A. Friedman, "Why Are Young Americans Killing Themselves?" January 6, 2020, *New York Times*, https://www.nytimes.com/2020/01/06/opinion/suicide-young-people.html?smtyp=cur&smid=fb-nytimes.

5. Kim Hjelmgaard, "Iran OKs bill calling U.S. military, Pentagon terrorists after Qasem Soleimani killing," January 7, 2020, *USA TODAY*, https://www.usatoday.com/story/news/world/2020/01/07/iran-says-u-s-military-pentagon-terrorists-qasem-soleimani-killing/2830669001.

6. Arian Campo-Flores and Jennifer Calfas, "Another Powerful Earthquake Jolts Puerto Rico," January 7, 2020, *Wall Street Journal*, https://www.wsj.com/articles/puerto-rico-struck-by-magnitude-6-5-earthquake-11578389737?mod=hp_lead_pos2.

7. Meredith Colias-Pete, "Indiana steelmaker ArcelorMittal denies manipulating tests after toxic spill killed thousands of fish," January 7, 2020, *Chicago Tribune*, https://www.chicagotribune.com/suburbs/post-tribune/ct-ptb-env-fishkill-arcelormittal-redos-st-0107-20200107-p2frywilibg2pf7bcfz64y6vsu-story.html.

8. Allison McNearney, "Hey, Babylon, Nineveh Wants Its Hanging Gardens Back: The Truth of an Ancient Wonder," January 27, 2018, *The Daily Beast*, https://www.thedailybeast.com/hey-babylon-nineveh-wants-its-hanging-gardens-back-the-truth-of-an-ancient-wonder.

9. *New Living Translation Illustrated Study Bible* (Carol Stream, IL: Tyndale, 2015), 1566.

10. Jonathan Jones, "'Some of the most appalling images ever created' I am Ashurbanipal review," November 5, 2018, *The Guardian*, https://www.theguardian.com/artanddesign/2018/nov/06/i-am-ashurbanipal-review-british-museum.

11. Joshua J. Mark, "Assyrian Warfare," May 2, 2018, *Ancient History Encyclopedia*, https://www.ancient.eu/Assyrian_Warfare.

12. Nancy DeMoss Wolgemuth, "God is at Work," Sermon, *Revive Our Hearts*, October 7, 2010.

13. James Swanson, *Dictionary of Biblical Languages with Semantic Domains: Hebrew (Old Testament)* 1997: n.p., print (retrieved on Logos).

14. Charles R. Swindoll, "Habakkuk," https://www.insight.org/resources/bible/the-minor-prophets/habakkuk.

15. Ann Spangler and Sherri McDonald, *Don't Stop Laughing Now: Stories That Tickle Your Funny Bone and Strengthen Your Faith* (Grand Rapids, MI: Zondervan, 2002), 50.

16. Ibid., 51.

17. Dale Hudson, "20 Funny Bible Quotes From Kids," Relevant Children's Ministry, www.relevantchildrensministry.com/2017/06/20-funny-bible-quote-from-kids.

18. *New Living Translation Illustrated Study Bible*, "The Plagues, Exodus 7:14–11:10" (Carol Stream, IL: Tyndale, 2015), 152.

19. *New Living Translation Illustrated Study Bible* (Carol Stream, IL: Tyndale, 2015), 729.

20. Nancy DeMoss Wolgemuth, "Man of Sorrows," Sermon, *Revive Our Hearts*, December 19, 2018.

21. John Piper, "Judas Iscariot, the Suicide of Satan, and the Salvation of the World," October 7, 2007, Desiring God, https://www.desiringgod.org/messages/judas-iscariot-the-suicide-of-satan-and-the-salvation-of-the-world.

22. "Three Babylonian Inscriptions About the Exile," March 22, 2019, https://biblearchaeologyreport.com/2019/03/22/three-babylonian-inscriptions-about-the-exile.

23. Beth Moore, "Daniel, Bible Study Book: Lives of Integrity, Words of Prophecy," Workbook edition (Nashville: LifeWay Press, 2006), 34.

Week 3

1. Corrie Ten Boom, bible.org/illustration/corrie-ten-boom-0.

2. Ibid.

3. Reconstruction after World War II, *Encyclopedia Britannica*, https://www.britannica.com/place/London/Reconstruction-after-World-War-II.

4. Nancy DeMoss Wolgemuth, "Trials That Reveal Your Heart: A Message Based on Habakkuk," Sermon, *Revive Our Hearts,* October 28, 2010, https://www.reviveourhearts.com/podcast/revive-our-hearts/trials-that-reveal-your-heart-1.

5. Martin Lloyd Jones, *From Fear to Faith: Rejoicing in the Lord in Turbulent Times* (Downer's Grove, IL: InterVarsity, 1953), 27–30. This book is a series of messages Dr. Jones preached immediately following World War II.

6. Ibid., 28.

7. The Bible Project, "Holiness," Animated, https://thebibleproject.com/explore/holiness.

8. "Habakkuk 1," Matthew Poole's Commentary, Biblehub.com, https://biblehub.com/commentaries/poole/habakkuk/1.htm.

9. "Kings Put Hooks in Their Lips," Bible History Online, https://www.bible-history.com/sketches/ancient/assyrian-king-lips-eyes.html.

10. "How long was the journey from Babylon to Jerusalem?", www.esv.org/resources/esv-global-study-bible/facts-ezra-7.

11. Malcolm Gladwell, *Outliers: The Story of Success* (Boston: Little, Brown and Company, 2008), 39–42.

12. "Average Time Spent Daily on Social Media (Latest 2020 Data)," Broadband Search, https://www.broadbandsearch.net/blog/average-daily-time-on-social-media.

13. Jessica Dickler, "Americans spend nearly two hours a day shopping online at work, study suggests," CNBC, December 11, 2018, https://www.cnbc.com/2018/12/11/americans-spend-nearly-two-hours-a-day-shopping-online-at-work.html.

14. Michelle Castillo, "Netflix Only Takes Up 8 Percent of the Time You Spent Watching Video, but the Company Wants to Change That," CNBC, July 17, 2018, https://www.cnbc.com/2018/07/17/netflix-small-portion-of-overall-watch-time-and-competition-is-stiff.html.

15. Amy Reiler, "Guess How Much Time You Spend Eating On An Average Day," *Food Network*, July 2015, https://www.foodnetwork.com/fn-dish/news/2015/07/guess-how-much-time-you-spend-eating-on-an-average-day.

16. Cheyenne Buckingham, "This Is Exactly How Much Time You Spend Thinking About Food," *Eat This*, January 31, 2019, https://www.eatthis.com/time-spent-thinking-about-food-study.

17. Nancy DeMoss Wolgemuth, "Revive Your Work," Bible Teaching, *Revive Our Hearts*, October 22, 2010, https://www.reviveourhearts.com/podcast/revive-our-hearts/revive-your-work-1. Emphasis added.

18. Jonathan Merritt, "America's Epidemic of Empty Churches," *The Atlantic*, November 25, 2018, https://www.theatlantic.com/ideas/archive/2018/11/what-should-america-do-its-empty-church-buildings/576592.

19. Robert Nicholson, "A Coronavirus Great Awakening?" *Wall Street Journal*, March 26, 2020, https://www.wsj.com/articles/a-coronavirus-great-awakening-11585262324.

20. Robert Jamieson, A. R. Fausset, and David Brown, *Commentary Critical and Explanatory on the Whole Bible* (Oak Harbor, WA: Logos Research Systems, Inc., 1997), print.

21. "Revive," Merriam-Webster, https://www.merriam-webster.com/dictionary/revive#other-words.

22. Timothy J. Keller, "A Covenant Relationship," *Gospel in Life*, September 9, 2007, https://gospelinlife.com/downloads/a-covenant-relationship-5548.

23. David Baker, *Nahum, Habakkuk, and Zephaniah: An Introduction and Commentary*, Vol. 27 (Downers Grove, IL: InterVarsity, 1988), print (retrieved on Logos).

24. "A Smoking Fire Pot," *Ligonier Ministries* (blog), https://www.ligonier.org/learn/devotionals/smoking-fire-pot.

25. In many parts of Scripture we see God's presence being represented by fire—the burning bush, the fire over the tabernacle, and so forth. Hebrews 12:29 tells us that our God is a "consuming fire." Some scholars believe the reason it is in a pot is to prophesy that the Israelite people would be unfaithful and would be in a boiling pot of pain and trouble in Egypt. If so, God is in the pot with them.

26. Donna VanLiere, *The Time of Jacob's Trouble* (Eugene OR: Harvest House, 2020), 272.

27. "What is on the sealed scroll in Revelation 5-8?", Stack Exchange (Chat), 2020, Hermeneutics.stackexchange.com/questions/6129/what-is-on-the-sealed-scroll-in-revelation-5-8.

28. G. K. Beale, *The Book of Revelation: A Commentary on the Greek Text* (Grand Rapids, MI: Eerdmans, 1999), print (retrieved on Logos).

29. Andrew Peterson, "Is He Worthy?" Centricity Music, 2019, Music Video.

Week 4

1. "Join the Easter Song in Aleppo, Syria!" *Vimeo* video, 1:07, April 8, 2019, vimeo.com/330599090.
2. Caleb Park, "Syrian Christians sing Easter hymn in touching video: 'Everyday we live the resurrection,'" Fox News, April 2019.
3. Don Carson, *A Syrian Theologian's Reflections on Habakkuk,* 1st ed. 2016, 12.
4. Ibid., 27.
5. Ibid.
6. Ibid.
7. "Yada`," https://www.biblestudytools.com/lexicons/hebrew/kjv/yada.html.
8. C.S. Lewis, *Letters to Malcolm: Chiefly on Prayer* (Boston, MA: Mariner Books, 2002), 11.
9. Chris Tomlin shared this story many times in public. It touched me and I thought it was fitting here. He tended to tell different parts of it from interview to interview. Here are two of them: https://hope1032.com.au/stories/culture/guests-and-artists/2017/chris-tomlin-reminding-us-of-home-in-a-broken-world/ and https://life965.com/2017/12/chris-tomlin-didnt-follow-dads-advice.
10. Nancy DeMoss Wolgemuth, "How to Show Strength and Dignity," podcast, *Revive Our Hearts*, March 20, 2012.
11. Timothy J. Keller, "Waiting & Living by Faith," podcast, *Gospel in Life*, May 10, 2009.
12. Erin Davis delivered this in a yet-unpublished message at Revive Our Hearts headquarters, November 2019. Permissions on file.
13. *The Westminster Collection of Christian Quotations*, compiled by Martin H. Manser (Louisville, KY: Westminster John Knox Press, 2001), 122.
14. "Suicide," Leading Cause of Death in the United States (2017), National Institute of Mental Health, https://www.nimh.nih.gov/health/statistics/suicide.shtml.
15. The Bible Project, "Word Study: Yakhal-'Hope'," YouTube video, 04:33, Posted December 7, 2017, https://www.youtube.com/watch?v=4WYNBjJSYvE.
16. "Hope" (February 4, 2020), Wikipedia, https://en.wikipedia.org/wiki/Hope.
17. Paul Mozur and Ian Johnson, "China Sentences Wang Yi, Christian Pastor, to 9 Years in Prison," *New York Times*, December 30, 2019 (updated January 2, 2020), https://www.nytimes.com/2019/12/30/world/asia/china-wang-yi-christian-sentence.html.
18. Joe Carter, "Persecuted Chinese Pastor Issues a 'Declaration of Faithful Disobedience,'" The Gospel Coalition (blog), December 17, 2018, https://www.thegospelcoalition.org/article/persecuted-chinese-pastor-issues-declaration-faithful-disobedience.
19. "Coronavirus-Prayer Requests From the Church in Wuhan, China," *Asia Harvest* (blog), https://asiaharvest.org/coronavirus-prayer-requests-from-the-church-in-wuhan-china/.
20. Donna VanLiere, *Finding Grace: A Memoir* (New York: Griffin, 2013), 161.
21. Elisabeth Elliot, *Suffering Is Never for Nothing* (Nashville: Broadman & Holman, 2019), 12.

Week 5

1. "Revival on the Island of Lewis: 1949–1952," *Beautiful Feet: 53 Revival Stories* (blog), romans1015.com/lewis-revival.
2. David Smithers, ed., "The Intercessors of the Hebrides Revival," Measure of Gold Revival Ministries (blog), evanwiggs.com/revival/history/hebpray.htm.
3. Duncan Campbell, "Revival in the Hebrides Islands," *The Revival Library* (blog), revival-library.org/index.php/pensketches-menu/historical-revivals.the-hebrides-revival.
4. Walter J. Chantry, *Habakkuk: A Wrestler with God* (Carlisle, PA: The Banner of Truth Trust, 2008), 64.
5. "Pride," Lexico, www.lexico.com/en/definition/pride.
6. Andy Mylin, "Psalm 23," Sermon, Centre Church, Pleasant Gap, PA, Summer 2019.

7. "Does a narcissism epidemic exist in modern western societies? Comparing narcissism and self-esteem in East and West Germany," January 24, 2018, PLoS One, a peer-reviewed, open, access journal, 2018, 13(1): e0188287, https://www.ncbi.nlm.nih.gov/pmc/articles/PMC5783345.

8. https://www.christianquotes.info/quotes-by-topic/quotes-about-pride.

9. This is my own definition based on the study of the idea of biblical fear over the course of many years. I started to formalize my thoughts when studying Psalm 25:14 and came to the Hebrew word fear—*yara or yirah*. After that I began to study all of the words' appearances in scripture and developed this definition to help me recall the meaning.

10. Attributed to Albert Einstein at https://medium.com/@cmmacneil/nov-30-2015-step-four-the-feared-moral-inventory-of-12-step-recovery-4932acda4448.

11. Nancy DeMoss Wolgemuth, "Choosing Brokenness," *Revive Our Hearts* (blog).

12. "Woe," Merriam-Webster, https://www.merriam-webster.com/dictionary/woe.

13. John Piper, *Battling Unbelief: Defeating Sin with Superior Pleasure* (Portland, OR: Multnomah, 2007), 92.

14. "Code of Hammarabi," November 9, 2002 (updated February 21, 2020), https://www.history.com/topics/ancient-history/hammurabi.

15. "*Damnatio ad bestias*," Wikipedia, last modified March 7, 2020.

16. Donald J. Wiseman, General Editor, *Tyndale Old Testament Commentaries: Nahum, Habakkuk and Zephaniah* (Downers Grove, IL: Intervarsity, 1988) (retrieved on Logos).

17. "Revival on the Island of Lewis: 1949-1952," *Beautiful Feet: 53 Free Revival Stories* (blog), https://romans1015.com/lewis-revival.

18. Mary Peckham, "The Hebrides Revival," March 27, 2018, message delivered at 2000 Heart Cry for Revival Conference, https://www.youtube.com/watch?v=zS2Gw4u_Tv4.

Week 6

1. Andrew Ward, *Dark Midnight When I Rise: The Story of the Jubilee Singers Who Introduced the World to the Music of Black America* (New York: Farrar Straus & Giroux, 2000), 5.

2. "Swing Low, Sweet Chariot," Wikipedia, https://en.wikipedia.org/wiki/Swing_Low,_Sweet_Chariot.

3. Victoria Emily Jones, "God Swing Down Low (Artful Devotion)," June 26, 2019, Art & Theology, https://artandtheology.org/2019/06/26/god-swing-down-low-artful-devotion.

4. *New Living Translation Illustrated Study Bible* (Carol Stream, IL: Tyndale, 2015), 1397.

5. Etta James, "Swing Low, Sweet Chariot," 18 Great Gospel Favourites, Prism Leisure, 2004. CD. Original lyrics and music widely credited to either Ella Sheppard or Wallace Willis.

6. Terry Wardle, *Some Kind of Crazy: An Unforgettable Story of Profound Brokenness and Breathtaking Grace* (Colorado Springs, CO: WaterBrook, October 2019), 114.

7. James Swanson, *Dictionary of Biblical Languages with Semantic Domains* (Hebrew: Old Testament), 1997, Print.

8. Shane & Shane, "The Lord is My Salvation (Live)," Hymns Live, Well House Records; BMI Broadcast Music Inc, 2019, CD. Words and music by Keith and Kristyn Getty, Jonas Myrin, and Nathan Nockels.

9. Blayne Alexander, "Boy released by kidnapper after singing gospel music," *USA Today*, April 23, 2014, https://www.usatoday.com/story/news/nation-now/2014/04/23/gospel-singing-kidnapping/8042195.

10. "Kidnapped 10-year-old warned not to speak. But what he does next has abductor set him free," NTDIN.tv, July 11, 2017, http://ntdin.tv/en/article/english/kidnapped-10-year-old-warned-not-to-speak-but-what-he-does-next-has-abductor-set-him-free.

11. The Hebrew word for body in Habakkuk 2:16 is *beten* which means stomache. James Swanson, Dictionary of Biblical Languages with Semantic Domains: (Hebrew Old Testament) 1997: n.p. Print.

12. Caleb & Kelsey Grimm, "It Is Well," Hymns Wise Music Group, a division of Sony ATV Publishing, 2019, CD. Original hymn lyrics by Horatio Spafford and composition by Philip Bliss.

13. Christy Nockels, "Head to Toe (The Armor of God Song)," Be Held: Lullabies for the Beloved, Keeper's Branch Records/The Fuel Music, 2017, CD.

14. Rich Mullins, "The Joy of Jesus" (featuring Matt Maher, Mac Powell, & Ellie Holcomb), Provident Label Group LLC, a unit of Sony Music Entertainment, 2017, Lyric Video.

15. "Theodicy," Merriam-Webster.com, https://www.merriam-webster.com/dictionary/theodicy?utm_campaign=sd&utm_medium=serp&utm_source=jsonld.

16. *New Living Translation Illustrated Study Bible*, (Carol Stream, IL: Tyndale, 2015), 1476.

17. Robert Jamieson, A. R. Fausset, and David V. Brown, *Commentary Critical and Explanatory on the Whole Bible* (Oak Harbor, WA: Logos Research Systems, Inc., 1997), print.

18. Ryan Saavedra, "China Quarantines 40 Million, 1,300+ Infected; Expert Predicted Coronavirus 'Pandemic' Could Kill 65 Million; U.S. Evacuation Underway in China," *The Daily Wire*, January 25, 2020, https://www.dailywire.com/news/china-quarantines-40-million-1300-infected-expert-predicted-coronavirus-pandemic-could-kill-65-million-u-s-evacuation-underway-in-china.

19. Jennifer Calfas, Chong Koh Ping, and Drew Hinshaw, "Global Coronavirus Death Toll Passes 81,000 as Some Lockdowns Tighten," *Wall Street Journal*, April 7, 2020.

20. Chelsea Gohd, "NASA animation shows global effects of Australia wildfires, hurricanes and more," Space.com, January 26, 2020, https://www.space.com/australia-fires-hurricane-global-effect-nasa-animation.html.

21. Barbara Starr and Jennifer Hansler, "Three Rockets Hit US Embassy Compound in Baghdad, US Official Says," CNN.com, January 27, 2020, https://www.cnn.com/2020/01/26/politics/rocket-hits-us-embassy-compound-baghdad/index.html.

PODCAST ANSWER KEY

PODCAST 1, page 14.

Habakkuk means to <u>embrace</u> or <u>embracer</u>.

The Power of Habakkuk's Poetry

1. Poetry requires us to get <u>intimate</u> with <u>God</u>.
2. Poetry is <u>pregnant</u> with <u>persuasion</u>.
3. Poetry is <u>beautiful</u>.
4. The <u>extra work</u> poetry requires results in <u>eureka moments</u>.
5. Poetry helps us <u>remember</u>.

Others Who Thought Habakkuk's Poetry Was Powerful

1. <u>God</u> wanted it <u>heralded</u>.
2. The <u>Apostle Paul</u> used it as <u>backbone</u> of <u>core doctrine</u>.
3. <u>Martin Luther</u> used it to get through <u>his</u> <u>questions</u>.

PODCAST 2, page 46.

WE ARE ALL IN <u>EXILE</u>.

The Babylonian <u>captivity</u> is a picture of something <u>supernatural</u>. We're all <u>longing</u> to feel like we are <u>home</u>.

5 Characteristics of God's Voice

1. He often says something that's <u>contrary</u> to my <u>nature</u>, but is never <u>a contradiction</u> to His.
2. He <u>confronts</u> my <u>sin</u>.
3. He speaks to me more <u>frequently</u> when I am <u>obedient</u>.
4. He tells me things <u>I didn't realize I knew</u>.
5. There is <u>weight</u> to His voice.

PODCAST 3, page 80.

Habakkuk used <u>questions</u> to talk to God. In doing so, he lived up to <u>His</u> <u>name</u>.

<u>Wrestler</u>	<u>Embracer</u>
<u>Hab. 1:1–4</u>	<u>Hab. 1:12–17</u>
<u>Combative</u>	<u>Clinging</u>

Two Responses To God's Prophecy

1. Embrace the burden and join the faithful in passing on the baton of remembrance.
2. Reject the responsibility and selfishly nurture the contagion of spiritual amnesia.

PODCAST 4, page 118.

If you want to hear God's voice through the hurt, you must climb into your watchtower and watch for answers.

Four Ways To Watch For God

1. Watching hopefully.
2. Watching obediently.
3. Watching faithfully.
4. Watching perspectively.

PODCAST 5, page 148.

1. Our call to live in faith is first introduced to us in contrast to pride.
2. Pride is the opposite of faith. You cannot move in the way of something if you're walking in the opposite direction.
3. We want to be proactive rather than complacent, we must enter into ongoing rigorous self-inventory.

Two Kinds of Pride

1. Belittling
2. Boasting

PODCAST 6, page 178.

Habakkuk hasn't started to fake it. Even as he moves into a place of praise, he remains honest. The righteous person who lives by faith still has something to sing about. God often delivers us through our trials not from them.

We will be amazed at how hard the trouble in this world can be.
We will be amazed at how good God can be in the middle of the trouble.

UNCOVER THE LIES

BREAK FREE WITH THE TRUTH

978-0-8024-1528-8   978-0-8024-1836-4   978-0-8024-1489-2

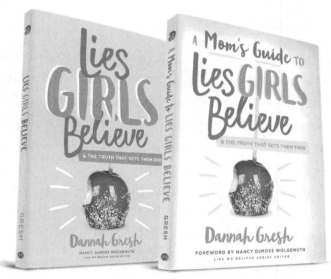

978-0-8024-1447-2   978-0-8024-1429-8

Abstinence isn't about not having sex—it's about waiting to have it right.

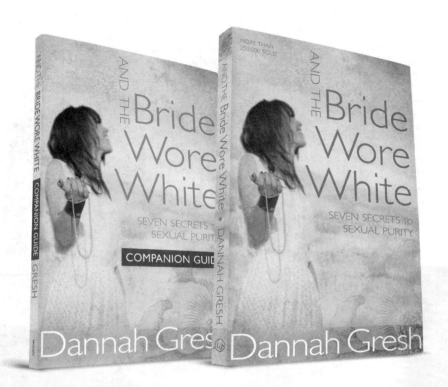

Bestselling author Dannah Gresh exposes Satan's lies about sex, gives a three-step plan to breaking off sinful relationships, and provides compassionate guidelines for healing. Since its release in 2000, *And the Bride Wore White* has touched the lives of over 250,000 young women.

AND THE BRIDE WORE WHITE: 978-0-8024-0813-6
COMPANION GUIDE: 978-0-8024-1289-8

also available as eBooks

MOODY
Publishers®

From the Word to Life®

Bible Studies for Women

IN-DEPTH. CHRIST-CENTERED. REAL IMPACT.

7 FEASTS
978-0-8024-1955-2

KEEPING THE FAITH
978-0-8024-1931-6

AN UNEXPLAINABLE LIFE
978-0-8024-1473-1

THE UNEXPLAINABLE CHURCH
978-0-8024-1742-8

UNEXPLAINABLE JESUS
978-0-8024-1909-5

THIS I KNOW
978-0-8024-1596-7

WHO DO YOU SAY THAT I AM?
978-0-8024-1550-9

HE IS ENOUGH
978-0-8024-1686-5

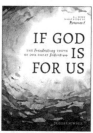

IF GOD IS FOR US
978-0-8024-1713-8

ON BENDED KNEE
978-0-8024-1919-4

HIS LAST WORDS
978-0-8024-1467-0

I AM FOUND
978-0-8024-1468-7

INCLUDED IN CHRIST
978-0-8024-1591-2

THE WAY HOME
978-0-8024-1983-5

A GREAT CLOUD OF WITNESSES
978-0-8024-2107-4

Explore our Bible studies at
moodypublisherswomen.com

Also available as eBooks

MOODY PUBLISHERS
WOMEN
BIBLE STUDIES

Experience Freedom Through God's Truth

Dig deep into God's Word with an online Bible study from True Girl!
Each study has a unique focus that will help you and the young
women in your life fight the world's lies as you grow closer to Jesus.
Join us for an upcoming livestream study, or access our library of
recorded studies that you can view on-demand.

Teachers You Can Trust

Dannah Gresh

Staci Rudolph

Erin Davis

< 900 BC   700 BC   600 BC   500 BC

930   Israel Divides

609

593

605

605–538

538

755

612–588